Decoding your life

By Janet D. Swerdlow

EXPANSIONS PUBLISHING COMPANY, INC.
P.O. BOX 12, ST. JOSEPH MI 49085 U.S.A.

Other books by Janet Swerdlow
Belief Systems Shattered
Belief Systems Shattered...Again
Practical Tips Volume I, II, & III
The True Reality of Sexuality (with Stewart A. Swerdlow)
The Hyperspace Helper: A User Friendly Guide
(with Stewart A. Swerdlow)

Decoding Your Life © 2005 Janet D. Swerdlow
(Formerly published as the *In Search of Yourself* series by Janet Dian—
Book 1: The Beginning © 1990, 1991, Book 2: Moving Forward © 1991, 1992,
Book 3: Finding the Balance © 1993, 1994)

Cover by: Richard Beardsley, Quixotic, LLC
Typography, and Book Layout by Lorraine Sarich, DBA L'OR Intuitives

Published by: Expansions Publishing Company, Inc.
                       P.O. Box 12
                       Saint Joseph MI 49085 U.S.A.
                       269-429-8615

                       ISBN 0-9740144-6-X

email: janet@janetswerdlow.com
Website address: www.janetswerdlow.com

Dedication
To the Original Life Support Group
Betty, Lena, Johanna, Jean, Fran, Arlo, Charlotte, Joyce,
Kathryn, Renee, Cyndi, and Josie

*Thank you all for teaching me how to be a teacher; for
encouraging me to put my words on paper; for your
sharing and caring; for your love and support; and best of
all, for so many wonderful memories.*

TABLE OF CONTENTS

Section III
Finding The Balance

INTRODUCTION

When I was in my early twenties, and alone on a farm in the high mountain desert of Eastern Washington State, I began my journey out of my "metaphysical closet." A close friend was having such heart-wrenching challenges with one of her children that I broke my inner code of silence to share some of these concepts with her. For the first time, she began to realize that the child was not a "blank slate" that she had somehow ruined. That was my first step to publicly teaching what I had known all of my life.

From there, I spoke to a friend who had a whole wheat bakery, quite a novelty in the early 1980s, especially in a small rural community. While she insisted a person's health had to do with nutrition, I taught her about mind-pattern analysis and introduced her to metaphysics. Our common interests soon joined us as fast friends, and we decided to place ads in all the papers in the surrounding communities for like-minds to gather. At our first meeting, we had over thirty people, many from towns over thirty miles away.

We had monthly meetings, as well as a smaller weekly study group that I taught. The study group included people from all walks of life and religions. Our group included Methodists, Mormons, Lutherans, Catholics, and even a Catholic nun! I never told anyone to leave his/her belief system, but to incorporate what I had to offer into their lives in a way that was comfortable. Everyone made dramatic changes and were so thrilled that they asked me to start writing my lessons down.

Every night before I went to bed, I wrote down one Universal Law that was applicable to everyone, and from each Law created one chapter in the book. The book was so big that people asked me to divide it into four books, which I did. The first three were published, but because of life circumstances, the fourth one on relationships never made it to press. This information is now included in the book that Stewart and I wrote together, *The True Reality of Sexuality.*

My *In Search of Yourself* series was published in Spanish as well as Chinese. Together, all three books in all three languages sold almost 40,000 copies worldwide. Rather than reprint the series as individual books, I decided to update some of the verbiage and put the books back together again. These books truly have been a labor of love for me. Written at the request of those people who studied with me, I believe this course of study to be simple, practical, and easy to implement with measurable results. As always, I ask my readers to keep an open mind, be willing to try, and most of all, enjoy the process.

Janet Swerdlow

SECTION I
THE BEGINNING

SLOWING DOWN

*"Learning from your present moment slows you down,
helping you to stop and think before you act."*

Hidden within every moment of your life are all the answers that you ever need. All you have to do is slow down long enough to let your moments teach you. Within each one, you state who and what you are. Within each one, your outer world reflects that statement back to you.

You may label your present moment very ordinary and mundane, but it is actually full of information that can take you into a whole new path of inner awareness. Each moment contains many, many clues that tell you who you are. Find your own clues right now.

Body Language

How are you sitting? Why did you choose that position? What inner thoughts and feelings are you expressing through your body language? Are you:

relaxed?

open and receptive?

open and skeptical?

closed and skeptical?

closed and uninterested?

tense?

Clothing

What clothes are you wearing? Why did you choose them? What do they express about your inner self? Are they:

dark and gloomy?

dark and grounding?

light and freeing?

light and spacey?

patterned and too busy?

striped and running you around in circles?

solid and strong?

solid and inflexible?

plaid and breaking up old patterns?

balanced or unbalanced?

Colors

What colors are you wearing? What do they tell you about your inner self?

Are you wearing:

green because it is a healing color, or because you are envious and jealous?

blue because it is calming, or because you are depressed?

yellow because you are wise, or because you are fearful?

brown because it is grounding, or because your thinking is muddy?

red because you are creative, or because you are angry?

purple because you are spiritual, or because you are selfish?

Your Home

What room are you in? What does it tell you about your inner self? Does it:

promote openness and communication?
promote privacy?

establish barriers?

feel comfortable and warm?

feel distant and cold?

Are the rooms in order?
Are they full of clutter?
<u>this</u> may reflect a mind that is full of clutter.

Does your home have closets and drawers that you think need to be cleaned out?
This may reflect a mind that is ready to let go of the past.

Does everything **have** to be in its place?
This may reflect a mind that is strict and inflexible.

Is there any dust?
This may reflect a mind that is afraid to let go of the past.

Are there any cobwebs?
This may reflect a mind that needs some mental exercise.

A Myriad Of Clues

By slowing down for just a few seconds, you have already found a myriad of clues that tell you who and what you are. When you take the time to stop and look around, you can find many more clues.

The way that you dress, the colors that you choose, the way you wear your hair, the arrangement of furniture and light in your home, the food that you eat, your yard, and your car are all clues that lead you into yourself.

Yes, they are exceptionally ordinary, but when you take the time to understand them, they become extremely interesting. Understanding them means understanding another level of yourself.

Understand Your Now

Remember when you were in school learning math? First, you learned to add and subtract. **Then** you learned to multiply and divide. You built one concept upon the other. In the same way, understanding what is happening **right now** is the first concept that you need. **Then**, you can understand the moment before the moment, or the moment after the moment.
Your present moment always holds the key to your past and future. Whatever you choose to express **right now** is a result of your past actions. Whatever you choose to express **right now** also sets your future in motion.

Whenever you have a question, look at your present moment. You will always find a clue that will lead you into an answer. Initially the clue may appear minute or insignificant, but it will direct you if you let it.

Learning from your present moment slows you down, helping you to stop and think before you act. It also teaches you to find your own answers, establishing a healthy, firm foundation upon which to build and grow.

Defining Your Space

*"If you react to situations through feelings that truly are not yours,
you need to find this out."*

Your own personal space consists of the area around you that contains who and what you are. This is your own personal energy field, more commonly referred to as your "aura." The basic shape of an aura is an oval, but there are as many variations on the shape as there are people.

For example, auras can be:
Lop-sided.
Long and skinny.
Short and fat.
Narrow and close to the body.
Wide and shooting out far from the body.
Close to the body and shooting out in some places.
Close to the body on the bottom and wide on top.
Narrow on top and wide on the bottom.

This gives you an idea of some basic variations. One variation is not "better" than another; each merely is an expression of a unique individual. The shape of your aura changes depending upon the experiences that you are going through at any particular time. Your aura can even change from day to day. As you grow, it goes through many changes.

Feel Your Aura

Determine the shape of your own aura by feeling it. Starting at your feet, move up your body with your thoughts. Feel how far out it goes, and how far up. Feel the space inside of your aura. Then, feel the space outside of your aura. You will be able to feel a difference.

The space inside of your aura feels like you. The space outside of your aura does not. On some level, you have always been aware of the shape of your aura. You are just taking the time to bring that awareness into your conscious mind.

Mixing Auras

You can also tell when your aura mixes with someone else's. For example, if someone stands too close, you say that they are in your "space." You feel his/her aura mix with your own. It makes you uncomfortable and you feel an invasion of your privacy. You intuitively want to take a couple of steps back to keep your auras separate.

Taking a couple of steps back will not always help. For instance, your aura may have places where it shoots out six feet from you. Or, you may be around someone whose aura shoots out six feet toward you. Taking a couple of steps back will not change anything. Furthermore, taking a couple of steps back is not always possible. You may find yourself at a crowded meeting or in the middle of a crowded shopping mall. In close quarters, you may feel uncomfortable without knowing why. The reason is because you mix auras with other people without being aware that this is happening.

Their auras are in your aura, and on some level of awareness you feel whatever is going on in their lives. Because most people try to express positive aspects while suppressing negative ones, negative feelings are often the most prominent in auras.

For example, on some level you feel the mood swings, relationships, financial status, home life, occupation, and stresses, as well as all the other feelings that surround others.

Whatever others feel may directly affect what you feel. You may begin thinking thoughts that did not originate in your head.

You may feel an invasion of your privacy, because on some level they feel what is going on in your life.

Automatic Energy Exchange

You may feel tired after being in a crowd of people. This is because you mix auras, and also unknowingly exchange energy with other people. Just as a heat exchange occurs when you mix hot with cold, you exchange energy with other people.

This is one reason why older people, or sick people, enjoy youth so much. They automatically draw the energy of the younger or healthier person. This is an automatic process and is not something they consciously make happen.

If you are in a crowd, and there are some tired people in it or ones that may not feel well, they automatically draw your energy to them. Because crowds usually contain many tired, busy people, you sometimes feel drained fairly quickly.

Be Aware Of Your Boundary

If you are aware of the boundary of your own aura, you can pull it in by willing it to do so with your thoughts. Just as you reach out and pull a physical object toward you with your hand, reach out with your thoughts and pull your aura toward you. Feel the boundary of your aura change.

Create A Bubble

Once you pull your aura in, place a clear bubble around it. This contains your aura within a specific boundary. All you have to do is take a second or two to visualize a bubble around your aura. Willing it to occur causes it to happen. This does not take place in your imagination. You actually create something with your thoughts.

The next time you are in a crowd, or among any group of people, consciously stop and take a couple of extra moments to pull your aura in and place a violet bubble around it.

You can do it once, or as many times as necessary to assure yourself that it is still there. Later when you are alone again, be aware of how you feel. Take a couple of seconds to determine if you are more comfortable and have more energy.

Family And Friends

Remember to use this tool when you are around family and friends. Maintain your bubble all the time because an automatic energy exchange takes place regardless of whom you are around. This does not make you have less feelings toward other people, but merely begins the sorting out process. You still feel, and the other person still feels.

The only difference is that you are able to correctly focus your energies. You are no longer distracted by the feelings that are present in each aura. And, your communication actually becomes clearer, more open, and more direct. People become more comfortable because they no longer mix auras with you.

Keep Your Space Separate

Almost everyone has some type of emotional clutter surrounding them. Keep your space separate to help sort and organize your own feelings. This is a basic beginning point for finding out who you are. If you react to situations through feelings that truly are not yours, you need to find this out. Defining your space allows you to do this.

REALISTIC EXPECTATIONS

*"As you learn to be gentle with yourself, you develop true compassion
and understanding for other people and their lives."*

One of the greatest pressures that you can put upon yourself is the perception of how you "should" be. You develop a list of rules for yourself that may be impossible to follow in practical terms. This list may be something that you have actually labeled, or, you may not even be aware that you have a list. The list that you use probably looks something like this:

I "should":

React to all situations calmly.

Never be angry, resentful, and/or bitter.

Always be understanding.

Be pleasant.

Speak patiently.

Have great relationships.

Be open and honest.

Be strong and supportive.

Always express love and peace.

Have clear direction in all situations.

The list can go on and on. When you consider what you expect of yourself, the pressure of who you think you "should" be can be overwhelming. You chastise and criticize yourself whenever you act differently from the person that you think you "should" be. Your efforts are admirable but not realistic.

You Are Dual-Natured

In reality, you contain both positive and negative aspects. You are dual-natured. When you concentrate on overemphasizing the positive to compensate for the negative, you ignore an integral part of yourself.

Negative Aspects Are Important

Ignoring negative aspects do not make them go away. Instead, you only bury them deeper and deeper into your body, subconscious mind, and personal energy field, or aura.

Negative aspects are important:

They are an integral part of life.

They are excellent teachers.

When you are determined to ignore them, you may not realize how often they are the missing link in many of your dilemmas. Basic behavior patterns almost always contain both positive and negative components somewhere. When you ignore the negative, these patterns can be virtually impossible to identify.

Understanding this allows you to fill in the missing links, thus identifying specific behavior patterns. Once identified, you can make informed decisions on how, and if, you want to change these patterns. Learn to move through the discomfort of the negative by viewing it as a positive growth experience.

Acknowledging the existence of negative aspects gives you permission to recognize them as they occur. As you recognize them, you can label them. Then, you can study your life piece by piece, and diagnose it without judgment or criticism. This allows you to examine yourself as you are, and work with what is. It moves you through your illusions, and places you into reality.

Please recognize that your study of self-awareness is a slow, methodical route to a balanced change within. You will learn to appreciate your strengths **and** weaknesses. Thus, your growth potential will be reached. Because you make small, balanced, incremental adjustments within, you can easily accept the changes. In turn, this means that any changes you decide upon are effective and long-lasting.

Acknowledge Who You Are

Acknowledging who you are activates a process of self-healing as you stop hiding from yourself. All that you are is now out in the open. This openness allows you to accept yourself for who you are, instead of constantly criticizing yourself for who you are not.

You Are Where You Are Supposed To Be

You are where you are supposed to be with the tools, knowledge, and experience that you have. Realizing this allows you to change your list to one with more realistic expectations. It is much more realistic to say:

I *sometimes:*

React to situations calmly, but sometimes do not.

Am angry, resentful, and/or bitter, but sometimes am not.

Am understanding, but sometimes am not.

Am pleasant, but sometimes am not.

Speak patiently, but sometimes do not.

Have great relationships, but sometimes do not.

Am open and honest, but sometimes am not.

Am strong and supportive, but sometimes need to be supported.

Express love and peace, but sometimes do not.

Have clear direction, but sometimes need guidance.

Be Gentle With Yourself

Changing your list helps you to be less strict with yourself. This develops a more gentle attitude toward who and what you are, and what you truly can expect from yourself with the tools, experience, and knowledge that you have. You develop more compassion and understanding for yourself.

You are not a "perfect" person or you would not be here. So, why are you expecting yourself to act like a "perfect" person? Striving toward growth is important, but do it in a way that is comfortable for you. Work within a realistic framework of expectations.

Everyone Is Learning

As you learn to be gentle with yourself, you develop true compassion and understanding for other people and their lives. Everyone is learning whether he/she consciously acknowledges it or not. There are many paths, and each one is made up of a variety of positive and negative experiences.

Everyone experiences whatever it is that he/she needs to lead that person deeper into his/her inner self, and deeper into God-Mind. No matter where anyone is in the evolutionary process, his/her path is just as difficult as yours, and just as important.

YOU HAVE THE ANSWERS

"You, along with your Oversoul and God-Mind, can
*find any answers that you **need**."*

The challenges in your life did not just happen. They evolved through a series of actions that you set up over a course of time. On some level of awareness, you created them, so that you could learn and grow from them.

Because you created them, you have the knowledge to dismantle them. All you have to do is work backwards.

When you are in the middle of a challenge, it can be difficult to assess where you are, how you got there, and what you can do to get out of it. You may relate to the old saying, "You can't see the forest for the trees."

Recognize Specific Actions

You need a tool to help you recognize the specific actions that have created your challenges. Once you know what those actions are, **then** you can determine where you are, how you got there, and what you can do to get out of it.

Affirmations are powerful and useful tools that bring specific answers to specific questions forward into your conscious mind. An affirmation is a statement that defines a course of action, or a state of inner being. Repeating affirmations many times by thinking, speaking, or writing can bring new avenues of action into your conscious mind.

Using Affirmations

Both your positive and negative actions almost always combine together into patterns that create your challenges. Recognizing this, the affirmations that you choose provide answers that you can accept and utilize.

As an example, you may be experiencing a difficult relationship with your son. Your first thought might be that you try your hardest, and you do not understand why he acts the way that he does toward you.

Slow down and remember that your outer world is a reflection of you. Then ask the question, "What am I doing that is being reflected back to me by my son?" No matter how hard you think, you may not be able to come up with an answer.

You Already Know

An affirmation can bring that answer into your conscious mind, because on some level of awareness you already know. Start with a basic affirmation that states the basic problem and your willingness to resolve it:

I am willing to release the conditions that create a negative relationship with my son.

To put the affirmation into motion, think of it throughout your day, speak it out loud if you wish, and most effectively, write it a minimum of ten times daily.

Because you are willing to release the conditions, they will surface up from your aura, up from your subconscious mind, and out of your physical body, where they have been buried. On their way out, they pass through your conscious mind. This identifies those conditions for you.

Positive And Negative Actions

Because both your positive and negative actions have combined into a pattern of behavior to create your present challenge, expect both positive and negative actions to surface into your conscious mind.

For example, you may learn that you tried to gain your son's love and approval by controlling and manipulating him. Wanting his love is a positive action. Your attempt to gain it through control and manipulation is a negative action. He resents your interference, and now he is rebelling.

You may learn that you always criticize and correct him to "make him a better person." Wanting him to be a better person is a positive action. Criticizing and correcting to make him one is a negative action. He may not appreciate that, and expresses his disapproval through actions against you.

Or, perhaps you are still angry with him over specific childhood incidents. You try not to feel angry at him. That is a positive action. But, on some level, your anger still exists. That is a negative action. On some level, he feels and reacts to your anger.

Remember, there is no need to judge or criticize yourself when you identify these patterns of behavior. Realistically, you are where you are supposed to be with the tools, knowledge, and experience that you have. Be thankful that you are facing these parts of yourself so that you can learn from them, release them, and make specific changes.

Release The Conditions

Now that you are aware of the conditions that create the negative relationship, release them with the following affirmation:

***I release the conditions that create a
negative relationship with my son.***

You may want to release specific conditions, because they also create other negative relationships. Use one or more affirmations from the following subset:

I am willing to release my need to be controlling and manipulative.

I am willing to release my need to criticize and correct.

I am willing to release my need for anger.

Prepare For The New

As those aspects are released, prepare for a new relationship with your son. Change your affirmation to the following:

I am willing to accept a positive relationship with my son.

To enhance that positive relationship, use this subset of affirmations:

I allow my son to be who he wants to be.

***I allow myself to have relationships
centered around positive experiences.***

As your relationship improves, continue to change your affirmation to fit your present:

I accept a positive relationship with my son.

And, finally, change it one last time to pull you into a positive relationship with your son:

I now have a positive relationship with my son.

A Part Of The Process

Initially, this may look like a lot of work, and, in a way, it is. But, your relationship did not get to be the way it is overnight. It developed over many years. So, take the time to effect a long-lasting change instead of looking for a quick fix. Eventually, you will enjoy searching out the conditions and making the changes. It is all a part of the process:

You create a negative relationship.

You dismantle the negative relationship.

You create a positive relationship.

Affirmations Bridge Gaps

You may also need to design a series of affirmations to bridge the gap between what is, and what you want to be. For example, if your body is experiencing illness, you may choose the following affirmation:

I have a healthy body.

You may **want** to believe that your body is healthy, and you may **try** to believe that it is healthy, but this is not your reality. If your body is not experiencing health, it may be difficult to convince your conscious mind that it is. You may feel an internal struggle as you try to convince yourself that it is healthy.

At the end of this chapter you will find an example of a series of affirmations for a healthy body that you can use to help bridge the gap between your current and future reality.

A Five Step Process

When you are working hard to find an answer to a challenge that has you baffled, there is a process of designing affirmations that will maximize their effectiveness. It consists of the following five steps:

1. Find out what conditions are causing your present situation.
2. Release the old conditions.
3. Prepare yourself to accept the new conditions.
4. Accept the new conditions.
5. Affirm your new condition.

Utilizing these steps prepare the soil to accept the seed. If the soil is not properly cultivated, fertilized, and watered, the seed will have difficulty taking root. This is an extremely effective process, and the results are long-lasting.

Writing Affirmations

The most effective way to utilize affirmations is to write them. Get a notebook with lots of paper, and allow yourself a few minutes every day to write the affirmation that you have chosen. If possible, set a specific time, such as first thing in the morning, or before you go to bed at night. Establish a routine that helps you follow through with your goals.

Writing affirmations may be a challenge in the beginning, but your results will encourage you. Experiment with different affirmations to find the ones that feel right at the time. Finding affirmations that work for you becomes easier with practice. There are some short and simple affirmations in the appendices that you might enjoy using.

Design Your Own

There is also a guideline for designing your own affirmations at the end of this chapter, followed by some examples. Start with the first one in the series, and write it a minimum of ten times daily. If you think about it during the day, repeat it silently or out loud.

When you feel comfortable that you have fully utilized the first affirmation, and have received answers that make sense to you, move on to the next affirmation in the series. In addition, work with the subset that you have developed. You will know when it is time to move on to the next one.

The more times that you write each affirmation, the faster you bring answers into your conscious mind. You may find that you do not have to use all five steps. You may be able to use two or three steps, depending on your challenge.

Affirmations Evolve

Eventually, your affirmations evolve on their own as you use the process. You do not have to think about the next step—it automatically occurs. One day, while writing your current affirmation, you may feel like changing it. You automatically flow with what is right for you—as a unique individual with a unique path into yourself.

Affirmations bring very immediate results. They teach you that you already have the answers. You, along with your Oversoul and God-Mind, can find any answer that you need. All that is necessary to get started is a few minutes a day, a piece of paper, a pen, and an open mind that allows you to try.

Guideline For Designing Affirmations

Using the following five step process, develop a series of affirmations that work for you. Start with the first affirmation, and when you are satisfied with the information that you have brought forward, *then* design your second one. When the second one has brought the answers forward that you need, *then* design your third, etc.

1. Find out what conditions are causing your present situation:
   I AM WILLING TO RELEASE THE CONDITIONS THAT CREATE...
      Make a list of those conditions as they come into your conscious mind.

2. Release the old conditions:
   I RELEASE THE CONDITIONS THAT CREATE...
      Develop a subset of affirmations.

3. Prepare yourself to accept the new conditions:
   I AM WILLING TO ACCEPT...
      Develop another subset of affirmations.

4. Accept the new conditions:
   I ACCEPT...

5. Affirm your new condition:
   I NOW AM/HAVE...

Affirmations For A Healthy Body

1. I AM WILLING TO RELEASE THE CONDITIONS THAT CREATE **ILLNESS**.

This affirmation brings the conditions that create illness into your conscious mind. Those conditions might be:

It gives me extra attention from family and friends.

It gives me a chance to talk about myself.

It teaches me how to take care of my body through negative learning.

2. I RELEASE THE CONDITIONS THAT CREATE *ILLNESS.*

You may need a subset of affirmations:
I release the need for negative attention.
I release the need to learn about my body in a negative way.
I release the need for (specific thought and behavior patterns that create my specific illness).

3. I AM WILLING TO ACCEPT A **HEALTHY BODY**.

You may need another subset of affirmations:
I am willing to accept positive attention.
I am willing to learn about my body in a positive way.
I am willing to change (specific thought and behavior patterns that create my specific illness).

4. I ACCEPT **A HEALTHY BODY**.

5. I NOW HAVE **A HEALTHY BODY**.

Affirmations For Abundance

1. I AM WILLING TO RELEASE THE CONDITIONS THAT CREATE **LACK**.

This affirmation brings the conditions that create lack into your conscious mind. Those conditions might be:

My mother told me I would never amount to much.
Other people experience abundance, but it won't happen to me.
I am not worthy of abundance.
I do not deserve abundance.

2. I RELEASE THE CONDITIONS THAT CREATE **LACK**.

Your subset of affirmations becomes:
I forgive my mother for her words.
I forgive myself for believing them.
I am a worthwhile and deserving person.

3. I AM WILLING TO ACCEPT **ABUNDANCE**.

Your next subset of affirmations becomes:
I am worthy of abundance.
I deserve abundance.

4. I ACCEPT **ABUNDANCE**.

5. I NOW EXPERIENCE **ABUNDANCE**.

Affirmations For Positive Relationships

1. I AM WILLING TO RELEASE THE CONDITIONS THAT CREATE **NEGATIVE RELATIONSHIPS**.

This affirmation brings the conditions that create negative relationships into your conscious mind. Those conditions might be:

I am controlling and manipulative.
I am complaining and criticizing.
I hold inner hostility toward people in my life.

2. I RELEASE THE CONDITIONS THAT CREATE **NEGATIVE RELATIONSHIPS**.

Your subset of affirmations becomes:
I am willing to release my need to be controlling and manipulative.
I am willing to release my need to complain and criticize.
I am willing to release my need to be hostile.

3. I AM WILLING TO ACCEPT **POSITIVE RELATIONSHIPS**.

Your next subset of affirmations becomes:
I allow everyone to be who each wants to be.
I allow myself to have relationships centered around positive experiences.

4. I ACCEPT **POSITIVE RELATIONSHIPS.**

5. I NOW HAVE **POSITIVE RELATIONSHIPS**.

INTO THE SILENCE

*"Meditation produces feelings that no one can ever
adequately explain with words."*

Meditation is the most versatile and flexible tool that you can take with you in search of yourself. Easy to use, it quickly becomes very personal, and allows you to touch into continually deeper levels of inner awareness. The process of going within automatically changes you and your reactions to your inner and outer worlds.

Meditation is a process that must be used in order to understand it. It produces feelings inside of yourself that connect you to who and what you are.

Meditation takes you beyond words and puts you in touch with the level of feeling. Because you are so accustomed to identifying with words instead of with feelings, the process of meditation appears elusive. It is actually a simple activity that only through definition has become complex.

The process of meditation allows you the opportunity to slow down long enough to refocus your attention from your outer to inner world. It pulls your concentration into one focal point and directs it inward. It allows you to sink deeper and deeper into your center, melding your conscious, subconscious, and superconscious minds with your Oversoul and God-Mind.

Concentration

Almost everyone has the skill of concentration. It develops as you go through life. It takes concentration to play a game of basketball, knit an afghan, study for a test, or work at a computer. Somewhere in your life, you are already applying the skill of concentration. To meditate, all you have to do is redirect your concentration from your outer to inner world.

Inner Pressures

There are many inner pressures that prevent you from meditating before you even begin. For example, sometimes even saying the word "meditation" can make you feel awkward. Telling your family that you need time alone to meditate may make you feel uncomfortable. Your involvement in a new activity may be hard for them to accept.

If they give you a difficult time, remember, this is their way of coping with something new in their lives. They feel uncomfortable, so they try to make you feel uncomfortable, too. If you give up your new activity, they will not have to deal with it.

Respect yourself enough to find time to meditate. Eventually, your family will respect your request for time alone and privacy.

Find A Time

Find a time during the day or evening that is comfortable for you. Do your best to meditate on a regular schedule. Just as your stomach prepares itself to eat around your regular mealtimes, your body and mind automatically prepare themselves as your meditation time approaches. Set a time limit that works for you, establishes a routine, and fits into your daily schedule.

Right now, you may feel enthused and decide to meditate thirty minutes a day. You have no trouble finding the time to meditate on the first and second day. On the third day, something happens to interrupt your schedule, and you never get to it. By the fourth day, you think that you "should," but that is as far as you get.

By now, your original enthusiasm is gone, and either you have to rekindle it or you never start again. Your total experience with meditation was sixty minutes. This means that your original enthusiasm could be converted to equal sixty minutes.

Spend Your Enthusiasm

Rather than spend those sixty minutes of original enthusiasm quickly in two days, a more productive way would be to meditate for twelve days at five minutes per day. Your original enthusiasm remains the same, but you can usually fit five minutes into your schedule. A five minute routine is easier to maintain. Leave yourself wanting more rather than sabotaging your good intentions right from the start.

Give yourself a couple of weeks to decide if meditation is something that you want to pursue. If it is, then increase your time to ten minutes a day. After a few more weeks, and you are still maintaining your meditation time, then increase it to fifteen minutes.

Fifteen minutes a day is a good amount of time to devote to meditation once you have an established routine. As time goes by, you may find your time automatically increasing. You may sit to meditate for fifteen minutes, and the next thing you know, twenty minutes have passed, or thirty. Never increase your time because you think you "should.". Only increase it when you genuinely want to.

Sit Quietly

Another inner pressure may be your inability to sit quietly. Sitting quietly can be more difficult than it sounds. For example, it is not always easy to sit quietly when you are involved in an active lifestyle. There are so many activities to catch your attention, sitting quietly is not usually top priority.

The only experience you may have with sitting quietly is as a disciplinary action from your parents. When you sit to meditate, the child within you wants to squirm around. On some level, you still react to your past experiences.

Your lifestyle and past experiences often prevent you from sitting quietly, and the collective unconscious does not give you much encouragement. Western society is material-oriented and expects you to produce something. It expects you to be able to justify your time to the outer world. You can count the number of pages read in a book or miles driven in a car. But what have you produced when you sit quietly? Your training teaches you to produce, and you feel strange when you do not have a physical justification to show for your inner activity.

Sitting quietly is a skill that must be developed and integrated into your lifestyle. There are some suggestions in the appendices to help if this is difficult for you.

The Primary Purpose Of Meditation

The primary purpose of meditation is to establish a direct link to your Oversoul and God-Mind by opening the doors between your conscious, subconscious, and superconscious minds. These doors are made of silence. Silence is the level of feeling. As these doors open, you begin to know by knowing.

Your conscious mind contains your present.

***Your subconscious mind contains your memories, moment
by moment, lifetime by lifetime.***

***Your superconscious mind provides the direct link to your
Oversoul and God-Mind.***

During meditation, allow yourself to sink continually deeper into silence, the level of feeling. Feel yourself expand into your center and beyond your physical body. As you alter your conscious state, there is a feeling of movement. This is the natural rhythm of the universe that expands and contracts.

Everything exists and nothing exists simultaneously within the silence. It is here that you connect with your Oversoul and God-Mind through the level of feeling. Your Oversoul gently pushes whatever you need to know through the doors of silence and into your conscious mind.

Connecting with your Oversoul can occur within seconds, or, it can take a long time. It depends upon your ability to sit quietly so that you can feel. You may be getting information now from your Oversoul without even being aware of it because you are unaccustomed to communicating through feeling. Feelings occur first, and then the words are attached to explain those feelings. The process must be slowed down and defined to repeat it at will.

Three Keys To Successful Meditation

There are three keys to successful meditation:

Start from where you are—
If sitting quietly for five minutes is difficult, then practice just sitting.
Move into the next steps when you feel comfortable doing so.

Do not expect too much—
This only puts pressure on you that you do not need.

Go with what you get—
There is always a reason for whatever is passing before you.

As an example, if you have wandering thoughts that will not stop, perhaps they are providing you with information that you previously overlooked—pay attention to them.

Breathe Correctly

Your breath is an important part of the process of meditation. Focusing your attention on your breath pulls your attention further inward. Because of this, it is important that you breathe correctly. As strange as it sounds, not everyone knows how to breathe just because they are getting air into their lungs.

Women are especially likely to breathe incorrectly. They often learn at an early age to hold their stomachs in so that they look thinner and more attractive. As a result, they often tend to breathe with their upper chest rather than utilizing the full capacity of their lungs.

To determine if you are breathing correctly, lay your hand on your stomach. When you inhale, your stomach will inflate. When you exhale, your stomach will deflate. If you are not breathing in this manner, practice filling your lungs from the bottom up, while lying down. Then practice breathing while sitting, standing, walking, etc. It is important to breathe correctly when you begin your practice of meditation.

When you have learned to sit quietly, and to breathe correctly, then experiment with the following guideline:

Guideline For Meditation

Gently bend and stretch to release any tension in your body.

Sitting in a comfortable chair, keep your feet flat on the floor, or,
Lie down, keeping your legs stretched out straight and untangled.

Position your hands palm up in a receptive position.

Keep your spine straight—

This allows for optimum energy flow through the primary energy centers that are aligned along it.

Close your eyes.

Visualize where the center of your being is located—
Notice that it is aligned along your spine.

Pull your attention in from your outer world by willing all of your thoughts into your center.

Stop and feel how safe it is to be in your center. Focus your attention on your third eye area—

Do this by placing a finger on your forehead between your eyebrows and look at it from the inside, keeping your eyes closed.

Breathe in from the top of your head to the base of your spine.

Breathe out from the base of your spine through the top of your head.

Feel your breath pull your concentration further inward. Watch your breath as it goes up and down, in and out—

Give it weight, color, and consistency.

Notice that your breath creates a vacuum that pulls you deeper into your center.

Eventually, as soon as you start the breathing process, your breath will automatically pull you into your center.

Allow your breathing to return to normal. Notice how calm and quiet you feel.

(Should you wish to do so, it is at this time that you will do your meditative work).

Remember the feeling so that you can touch into it throughout the day.

Open your eyes.

Many Levels Of Awareness

There are many levels of awareness in meditation, and as you experiment, you will find them. The first level contains your wandering thoughts. It is normal for your thoughts to wander. When they do, simply acknowledge that they are wandering, and release them up to your Oversoul. Go back to your breathing.

The deepest level is silence. Because this is the level of feeling, words are not necessary. In fact, there are no words that can adequately express what occurs in silence. It is something that you must experience to understand. At this point, suffice it to say that when you touch into silence, you have immediate understanding of whatever it is that you feel. As you go further into the process of meditation, you will understand.

Touching into silence for even a few seconds is progress. Those few seconds provide the trail to follow deeper within. In the middle are many levels of awareness. This is where you do your meditative work.

Work From Your Center

Your center provides a safe place from which to work, and it is here that you observe and evaluate yourself. It is a place where you are without judgment or self-criticism.

In your center, you can safely examine whatever you are outwardly expressing. You can make decisions about which behavior patterns you want to keep and which ones you are ready to discard. From here, you release anything that you no longer need up to your Oversoul. You can make any decision that you want while you are in your center.

Objectively Observe

When you meditate, assume the role of an objective observer. This allows you to sort and file the information that you collect from your experiences. To gather your data, ask the following questions as you review the experiences that pass before your inner eye:

How did I act and react?

How did other people act and react?

What did I learn?

What remains to be learned?

What will I do the next time I have the same type of experience?

What was my cumulative learning from the experience?

Remember, you are objectively observing, i.e., you are not criticizing or judging. You are only evaluating what exists in order to accurately interpret the data. Then, make a conscious decision about any behavior patterns that you wish to change.

As you evaluate, release all of your observations up to your Oversoul. Check every corner of yourself to see what emotions are surfacing. Instead of denying any negative emotions that you find, experience them. Express to your Oversoul whatever it is that you feel.

Acknowledge All Emotion

Never suppress, ignore, or deny any emotion. You cannot release it unless you recognize that it exists. As long as you stay in your center, you are safe. You are accustomed to suppressing your negative emotions, because in the past it was too easy to let them control you.

From your center, as an objective observer who studies the subject, watch any part of you that contains negative emotion. Observe that it is a part of you, but it is not you. Remember, it can teach you if you let it.

Allow it to express its feelings as you watch from your center. When it is finished, pass it out of yourself by releasing it up to your Oversoul.

Learn To Know By Knowing

Return any information that surfaces into your conscious mind during meditation without explanation to your Oversoul. Your goal is to know by knowing. If you retain unexplained information, you tie yourself to a level of guessing. You want to pass into deeper levels of awareness so that you have an instant explanation for any information that you receive.

Meditation Suggestions

The following examples are what you can do while meditating:

Ask for guidance.

Clean out painful experiences.

Clean out pleasant experiences to make room for more.

Heal your mental, emotional, physical, and spiritual bodies.

Ask that healing be sent to all life forms in accordance with their needs and the wishes of their Oversouls.

Explore ideas.

Relax.

Review and release your daily life so that you do not build a storehouse of experiences you no longer need.

Allow other lifetimes to surface when it is appropriate, and when they have specific meaning to you.

Enter into silence, the level of feeling.

Be selective of how you spend your meditation time. Decide what is important for you to know. Ask for guidance from your Oversoul—and pursue that course of action.

Meditation Experiences Are Unique

Each person has different experiences during meditation. All experiences are equal in importance. No one has a "better" experience than anyone else. While meditating you may experience color, lights, sound, taste, smell, or pictures. Someone else may not. This does not mean that your experiences are better. It only means that each person is a unique individual on his/her own unique path to God-Mind.

Your goal is to move through the color, lights, sounds, tastes, smells, and pictures into continually deeper levels of awareness, into silence. This is the level of feeling that allows you to know by knowing by melding with your Oversoul and God-Mind. How you do that is very personal, and it is up to you and your Oversoul to determine how you will accomplish it.

Incorporate Your Learning

Your learning from your meditations automatically incorporates itself into your daily living. For example, if you experience calmness during meditation, stop and touch into it throughout the day. No matter how hectic the pace of your outer world, pull yourself into your center and survive that pace without having it pull you apart. Walk through your outer turmoil knowing that it only exists for you to learn about yourself.

Your learning extends into other areas of your outer world as well, such as:

Your concentration improves in every area of your life.

You observe your daily actions with less criticism and judgment—
   This allows you to be more gentle with yourself.
   This allows you to become more acceptable to yourself.

You understand instead of criticize and judge the actions of other people.

You release your experiences to your Oversoul as they occur, no longer carrying unnecessary vibratory imprints with you.

Your aura becomes cleaner and clearer.

You become more relaxed.

Your body looks younger.

Your body functions more efficiently.

You stop reacting to your present through your past experiences.

Your ability to communicate with your outer world improves.

You acknowledge and understand inner communication as it occurs.

Meditation also teaches you to quiet your thinking mind. A quiet mind means a clear mind. A clear mind is much more perceptive and accurate in its observations and evaluations.

Understand The Process

The more you work with the process of meditation, the more you understand what meditation is. Meditation produces feelings that no one can ever adequately explain with words. You must experience it to understand the feelings that it produces. Then, you can go back and say, "I know what you are talking about." The knowledge becomes yours because you have experienced it and you have learned through direct awareness.

WHAT IS GOD-MIND?

"You learn about the microcosm, you learn about the macrocosm.
You learn about the macrocosm, you learn about the microcosm."

All that is comes out of God-Mind. You are a part of God-Mind that determines the totality of God-Mind. You are a microcosm of the macrocosm. Your basic building blocks come out of God-Mind.

For comparison, think about all the shapes that water can take:

Water is liquid—

Yet, it can also become ice, steam, or gas depending upon the rate of vibration of its atoms and molecules.

The substances look entirely different to the naked eye.

Yet, they all clearly originate from the same basic building blocks.

In the same way, you, your Oversoul, and God-Mind are all the same, basic neutral energy.

God-Mind Is Neutral Energy

God-Mind is neutral energy that is in the process of explaining Itself by experiencing Itself. Out of God-Mind was birthed all that is seen and all that is not seen. All that God-Mind provides acknowledges the existence of God-Mind.

God-Mind is in a continual process of experiencing God-Mind. God-Mind is rearranging God-Mind to answer the questions:

What am I?

What functions can I perform?

What shapes can I take?

What colors am I?

How deep am I?

How high am I?

What do I feel?

How many ways can I feel it?

Everything Is An Expression of God-Mind

As you practice the process of meditation you automatically understand that everything is an expression of God-Mind. Through direct awareness, you feel a connection with All That Is. This connection allows you to feel a Oneness with the Earth, the sky, and the sea; with plants and trees; with animals; and with other people.

You feel that Oneness pulling you into Itself. And, you understand what that Oneness is. Direct awareness is teaching you about God-Mind. You feel "I am a part of God-Mind; I am a part of All That Is."

As an example, the ocean may be used as an analogy to God-Mind. You are not the ocean (God-Mind), but you are a wave upon the ocean. You are very connected to it, with the potential to experience it by blending with it. Understanding the ocean begins by analyzing one drop of water. In the same way, understanding the microcosm, you, deepens your understanding of the macrocosm, God-Mind.

The Word "God"

Sometimes the word "God" makes people feel uncomfortable. Sometimes, religious upbringing is the reason that people feel uncomfortable. Sometimes, the reason is because "the name of God" has been used to justify many negative actions, such as war and violence. The vibrations from those actions have gone out into the collective unconscious and stuck to the word "God."

When people hear the word "God," they may feel the injustices that have been associated with its use. They may be reacting to the actions surrounding the word, rather than to the word itself. "God" is actually a pure and clear word that has lost some of its clarity through use.

You Are A Story

As a part of God-Mind, you are a unique set of experiences that continues to answer the question, "What is God-Mind?" You are a story waiting to be told, and you have the ability to tell your own story.

It would be very boring if you sat down to read a novel whose first page said, "The man was murdered." and whose second page said, "The butler did it. The end." The reasons you read the novel are for entertainment, to learn strategy, and to challenge your mind. You like putting together the clues and matching your mental abilities against the author's. You want to know all about the beginning, the middle, and the resolution. Each part of the novel is equally important.

The same is true of your life. It contains many chapters with beginnings, middles, and resolutions. Some chapters are still in progress and are unresolved. You may be avoiding the difficult chapters by looking the other way and hoping they resolve themselves. Just as you read a novel for intrigue, challenge, and entertainment, you set up your own personal story in the same way, for the same reasons.

Do You Choose Pain And Suffering?

Why would anyone choose to put pain, suffering, misery, or discomfort into their lives? Why would actors or actresses choose any role but a happy one? Why would they want to make people sad, or scare them? Why would they want to portray someone with mental or physical handicaps?

The answer for them is the same as it is for you: learning, growth, and experience. They want to see how they feel, act, and react, and they want to see how other people feel, act, and react.

You are here to experience, and experience means learning and growth. Becoming comfortable in a pattern of behavior that you no longer need can be easy, because moving out of it means moving into the unknown. The unknown can be frightening, even if it is a change for the better.

Pain, suffering, misery, and discomfort often move you when nothing else will. When you are uncomfortable enough, you opt to change something. It could be a minor, or a major, change but it always denotes learning and growth.

There are perks to pain, suffering, misery, and discomfort that you may not consciously recognize. For instance, they often provide the avenue for extra attention, sympathy, caring, and tenderness that you might not otherwise receive, or perhaps not even feel that you deserve. Stop and identify the benefits that your pain brings you.

Giving Your Power Away

Giving your power away by letting someone else tell you how and what you are, satisfies your instant curiosity. But, after that is gone, you have an empty feeling because you did not have the opportunity, or the satisfaction, or the thrill, of finding the knowledge that is deep within you.

Allowing other people to give you answers that you are capable of finding, provides a buffer that keeps you from becoming too involved with yourself. It keeps discomfort at a distance. Once it is close, you have to feel it and deal with it, and you may not be ready to do that yet.

Let other people act as a catalyst to help direct you, but do as much as you can on your own. When it is necessary, ask for only enough information to give you a boost so that you can do some more.

If you do decide to give your power away, then at least do so in conscious awareness.

Recognize and label what you are doing. When you are ready, take back your power. Use it to delve into yourself and read your own story.

There Are No Failures

Your life does have meaning within itself, and in relationship to the overall purpose of human drama. There are no failures, only circumstances that show you your strengths and weaknesses. Acknowledge these circumstances for what they are: tools that you have developed for yourself. Recognize that others have had these same experiences before you. More will have them after you have passed through them. You are never alone in your learning.

Your Experiences Come From God-Mind

All of your experiences come from God-Mind. You can choose to understand or not understand what is happening to you. But, it will happen anyway. Asking questions and objectively evaluating yourself from every perspective allows you to flow with your experiences.

You may still have the same experiences, but you understand and learn from them. You agree to them, knowing that you will be stronger and wiser when they are completed. You will not fight them, but accept them. This allows you to move with and through them, and on into the next one, knowing that each experience continues to explain you to yourself, and in turn, God-Mind to God-Mind.

Explore Who You Are

To understand the experiences that have made you who and what you are, be willing to explore who you are. Walk through your fears of the unknown, realizing that you are afraid, but that you are willing to try. Appreciate every experience, slowing down long enough to give every moment equal meaning and importance.

Meditation gives you the opportunity to develop a safe, quiet place to make accurate evaluations about who and what you are; a place to evaluate your strengths, your weaknesses, and your potential. A place where you can learn about yourself.

The more you learn about yourself, the more you appreciate yourself. You realize that you are the most fascinating and interesting person that you know.

The more that you appreciate yourself, the deeper you are able to go during meditation. The deeper you go, the more you learn about God-Mind; the more you learn about God-Mind, the more you learn about yourself.

The circle will perpetuate itself if you let it:

You learn about yourself; you learn about God-Mind.
You understand the microcosm; you understand the macrocosm.

You learn about God-Mind; you learn about yourself.
You understand the macrocosm; you understand about yourself.

Your ability to access knowledge is only limited by your willingness to move.

42

WHAT ARE YOU?

*"As a microcosm of the macrocosm, you are
individualized, neutral energy."*

During meditation you are aware that you are moving into places where your physical body cannot go. You understand that there is more to you than the physical body. You, as a microcosm of the macrocosm, are individualized neutral energy.

As energy you do not have arms and hands, or legs and feet. If you could look directly into the sun on a bright day, what you would see looks similar to what you actually look like. Ask to be shown what you look like during meditation.

Through inner awareness, you understand that you **have** a physical body, but you are **not** your body. Your physical body came from the bodies of your biological parents. Their bodies provided the avenue for you to enter into this dimension. Their bodies are the parents of your **body**, but they are not **your** parents.

The beings whom you call "Mom" and "Dad" have chosen to experience this lifetime with you. They may or may not be your biological parents in other lifetimes. Regardless, the learning that they give you in this lifetime is important.

Oversouls

The neutral energy that is called God-Mind is the equivalent of your grandmother/grandfather. Out of God-Mind came smaller portions of neutral energy called Oversouls. Oversouls also look similar to the sun on a bright day, but are much larger than you. Every person has an Oversoul. The equivalent of a mother/father, it is where **you** come from. It is your parent. Your Oversoul remains the same lifeline after lifeline. Your Oversoul is your point of origin out of God-Mind.

Your Oversoul also provides the intermediary link between God-Mind, a vast energy, and you, a small portion of that vast energy. Your Oversoul is a type of buffer between you and God-Mind. For example, you could not plug your kitchen toaster directly into an electric generator at a dam. The wattage from the electric generator would be too powerful, and would burn out the toaster.

Instead, you plug your toaster into a smaller wattage through an electrical outlet in your home. If you compare yourself to the toaster and the electric generator to God-Mind, you understand why you need the electrical outlet, or, your Oversoul.

Everything has an Oversoul for effective communication with God-Mind. There are Oversouls for the mineral kingdom, the plant kingdom, and the animal kingdom, as well as humankind. There are many Oversouls for each group. For example, one Oversoul is the parent of many men and women.

Each Individual Is Important

Each individual is important to its Oversoul. Personal identity is not lost, but enhanced. Each individual consists of unique experiences that contribute to the whole. Put another way, it is similar to the cells and organs in your body. Each cell and group of organs in your body has a special role. Your heart contributes something that your liver does not, and vice versa. Your body does not need two hearts or two livers, but one of each to function efficiently.

Each individual that belongs to the same Oversoul contributes his/her own unique experiences. For example, occupations, family and social relationships, and emotional experiences vary. Each individual contributes something that the others do not. As your Oversoul gathers your experiences and understanding, it passes them on to God-Mind. In this way, God-Mind continues to explain God-Mind by experiencing God-Mind.

God-Mind Needs To Experience God-Mind

You may wonder why God-Mind needs to experience God-Mind to explain God-Mind. Perhaps you can relate to the following analogy. You may love to swim. Sitting at home, in your easy chair, you know a lot about swimming. You know how the water feels, how your body feels, and how you feel.

You can think about swimming all you want, but it is not quite the same as actually swimming. If it were, you would never leave your easy chair. Swimming produces feelings that must be experienced. Only when you have experienced swimming can you adequately explain what it is. In the same way, God-Mind needs to experience God-Mind to explain God-Mind.

Your Oversoul Knows Your Life

Your Oversoul knows the entire picture of your life, from the beginning to the end. You are usually only aware of a portion of your life. This allows you to focus on the present moment in order to learn as you go. If you knew the outcome of your experiences, you would discount the importance of the present moment.

Making A Contract

Between lives, you make a contract with yourself and your Oversoul. This contract decides the general direction that your life will take to provide the learning that you need to fulfill your commitments to yourself, your Oversoul, and God-Mind. You are then born into those circumstances that allow you to complete that contract if you choose to complete it.

You always have free will to change your mind, but sooner or later, you will have to finish what you start. It is in your best interest to take a deep breath and move into your life.

You enter into this world without conscious knowledge of this contract. If you knew your life experiences in advance, you might be overwhelmed, or you might try to change it. However, as you grow, you develop the necessary skills to meet the challenges that come your way.

You may wonder why you would have agreed to your current challenges. You sign up for your life experiences in the same way that you sign up for any school. For example, in high school, you decide on a career as an engineer. At this time, you plan your college program. Once you are actually in college, you may find that some courses are more difficult than you anticipated. Yet, you still know that you need them to become an engineer. In the same way, there are going to be some difficult moments in your life, but what you learn from them prepares you for your future.

You Are Connected By A Channel

There is a clear, elasticized channel that connects you to your Oversoul. On some level of awareness, you may already be communicating with your Oversoul, depending upon the contract that you agreed to before you were born. You can open this channel through meditation and prayer, and develop conscious communication with your Oversoul.

Conscious Communication

The primary way that you now consciously communicate with your Oversoul is through physical death. You may have heard stories of people going through purgatory when they die. What they are actually doing is relaying their lifetime of experiences to their Oversoul so that together they can evaluate their life: what they learned and what remains to be learned. At this time, they start formulating the contract for their next lifeline.

Sometimes, you may even compile many lifelines before you share them with your Oversoul. This means that you and your body are full of vibrations from past experiences that you no longer need.

You can consciously share your experiences with your Oversoul now. Rather than accumulate them for one or more lifelines, you can release the vibrations of your experiences as they occur. As you do so, you become cleaner, lighter, and more flexible. This allows your mental, emotional, physical, and spiritual bodies to function more effectively because they are no longer bogged down with weight that they no longer need.

Conscious communication with your Oversoul means assuming more responsibility for your personal development. This gives you the chance to modify the contract that you agreed to many years ago, before you were born.

Instead of waiting until after-the-fact to share your life with your Oversoul, you can share it now. As an active participant, state the reasons why your life should or should not follow a particular course of action. Become an active partner in your own growth.

Use The Lines Of Communication

Although your Oversoul establishes an effective link between you and God-Mind, you can also share your life directly with God-Mind. There is a hierarchy, but you may use it however you like. As a comparison, you may sometimes wish to talk to your grandparents as well as, or instead of, your parents. The lines of communication are always open.

Your Oversoul helps you learn, and is always available. It is your partner as well as your parent. Ask it to guide you into your potential to continue experiencing all that is important to your individual growth. Allow it to direct you into even deeper levels of inner awareness.

Experiment And Question

The concept of Oversouls is touched upon in various esoteric writings. Determine for yourself if the concept is valid. Experiment with the ideas presented, and decide if they make sense. Gather the data, and evaluate it for yourself. Ask what an Oversoul looks and feels like during meditation. And remember—keep an open mind and be willing to try.

INNER COMMUNICATIONS

*"Discover on your own ways that your Oversoul
can work with and for you."*

Before you learn how to communicate with your inner world, it is important to first understand how you communicate with your outer world.

Psychic Energy

Definition: *Psychic energy is your own personal energy. It flows back and forth and is horizontal. It is not good or bad, it just is.*

Psychic energy moves the physical body and helps with communication in the outer world. For example, psychic energy is used to talk, walk, listen, digest food, etc. As psychic energy is depleted, the amount available to the physical body diminishes.

When you talk, you feel energy flow out of your mouth. You feel it flow horizontally. When you listen, you feel the horizontal energy of the other person hit your ears. Sometimes, on some level, you may almost feel invaded when people talk to you. You feel the harshness of the energy that they send toward you.

Mixing Auras

Because psychic energy moves back and forth, it passes through your aura and the vibratory imprints of your accumulated past experiences. When you talk to someone he/she feels more than your words. On some level of awareness he/she also feels the feelings of your past experiences.

Passing through your aura, your words pick up the feelings of your past experiences. Then, as this energy moves into another person's aura, it picks up the feelings of his/her accumulated past experiences. The energy that eventually hits his/her ears is loaded up with all of these feelings. This mixes auras and creates discomfort on some level of awareness.

Feel The Energy

Stop and feel the energy that people use when they communicate. Feel the horizontal flow of the energy as it moves back and forth. Feel the energy of your own words as you talk.

Universal Energy

Your physical body needs your psychic energy to function. Maximize the amount of psychic energy available to it by working with universal energy.

Definition: *Universal energy is energy that is available to everyone. It flows up and down and is vertical.*

Universal energy allows you to communicate with your Oversoul. You are connected through the top of your head to your Oversoul by a clear, elasticized channel. Using universal energy, communication flows vertically between you and your Oversoul through this channel.

Because universal energy flows through this channel, it passes through a different area of your aura. This creates a cleaner, clearer energy.

Prepare The Channel

The breathing work in meditation prepares you to use universal energy. It starts your energy moving up and down.

With your breath, continue to open and expand the channel. As you exhale, send it all the way up the channel into your Oversoul. As you inhale, bring your breath back down the channel to the base of your spine.

If you see or feel any dark, accumulated debris, use your breath as a scrub brush to clean it out. As you move your breath up and down, pass the loosened debris on up the channel to your Oversoul.

Feel The Channel

Working with your breath also deepens your level of inner awareness. As an example, feel the difference in the substances that your breath passes through. Starting at the base of your spine, exhale up and out of your body. Feel your breath pass through the space that contains your physical body. As your breath passes out the top of your head, feel the space that sits directly on top of your head. This space contains your thoughts.

It feels different than the space that holds your physical body. The next space that you pass into is the channel that connects you to your Oversoul. It also has a specific feeling.

It feels like "empty space" when compared to the space that holds your thoughts. While your breath is in the channel, will yourself outside the channel for a moment. Feel the difference between being inside and outside the channel.

Move Into The Channel

To communicate with your Oversoul, push through your physical body, out the top of your head, through your own thoughts, and into the channel. When you push up high enough, you can communicate with your Oversoul.

In the beginning, it may be difficult to know that anything is happening. Your communications may be so subtle that you are not able to separate them from your own thoughts and feelings. That is why it is important to push up above the space that contains your own thoughts.

If you do not, then you may have difficulty distinguishing your own thoughts and feelings from the feelings of your Oversoul. Your reasoning mind tries to talk you out of whatever it is that you feel. The more you use the channel, the more perceptive you are to the communications that flow down it.

More Accurate Observations

Moving your energy up and down, instead of back and forth, enables you to examine your life with greater accuracy. No longer looking horizontally through your accumulated vibratory imprints, you look at it from above, as an objective observer. This means you make more accurate observations.

Activate The Process

As you objectively observe, pass your data up the channel to your Oversoul. Ask your Oversoul to evaluate it and return the conclusions to you. Continue to move the energy up and down, even if you are unsure that anything is happening. Using the process activates the process. Eventually, you understand it through direct awareness. Then you can say, "I know by knowing; now I understand what I was reading about".

Your data goes up the channel, and the evaluations come back down. Each time you use the channel, you push your energy up. As you utilize the channel, you find that you pass through your own conclusions first. With practice, you feel the differences between your own conclusions and those of your Oversoul.

Feel The Conclusions

You feel your own conclusions in the space above your head. You feel the conclusions of your Oversoul in the area of "empty space" above your thoughts. Sometimes it is difficult to push up high enough to access the conclusions of your Oversoul. You like your own so well that it is easy to stop with them. Move through them, going up higher into the channel.

"Hunches"

You may already be using universal energy and communicating with your Oversoul without being aware of it. At some time during your life you have probably followed a "hunch" with successful results. Usually, you label these hunches "intuition".

You may have said, "I had a **feeling** to do thus and so, and I'm glad I did". Sometimes, you have a **feeling** to do something, but you let your reasoning mind talk you out of it. Then, after-the-fact, you tell yourself that you "should" have done thus and so because you had a **feeling** that told you to.

Those **feelings** are communications from your Oversoul, but, without awareness of the process, you cannot repeat the experience at will. You have to passively wait for another "hunch".

You are now slowing down the process, defining it, and labeling it so that you can use it at will. Using the process allows you to actively go within and get a "hunch" whenever you need one. Using the process refines it so that your "hunches" become more accurate.

Communicate With Other People

Using universal energy to communicate with other people is clean and efficient. Feel your words pass up the channel to your Oversoul whenever you speak to someone. Observe that your energy flows vertically rather than horizontally.

Ask your Oversoul to pass your words on to the other person's Oversoul, down his/her channel, and through the top of his/her head. Visualize the process happening. This keeps your words clean and their meaning clear.

Whenever you want to talk to someone, silently speak first through your Oversoul, even if it is only to say hello. This catches the person's attention on another level, and redirects their concentration towards you. It prepares that person for your conversation before it occurs.

Before talking to someone, always silently speak through your Oversoul first. Another individual does not have to be physically present for you to talk to him/her. On some level of awareness the person receives your message, thus preparing him/her for your conversation.

Because he/she receives your message on another level, fewer spoken words are necessary. You might not even have to say much at all. The other person may address your concerns or answer your questions before you speak.

Ask Your Oversoul To Help

Whenever anyone speaks to you, visualize a giant hand inside of your head scooping the words up the channel to your Oversoul. Ask your Oversoul to clean up the words so that you understand the feeling behind them.

When you read, feel the written words go up the channel. Ask your Oversoul to explain the material as it directly relates to you. Whenever you want to remember something, pass that information up the channel, and ask your Oversoul to remember it for you.

Pass all of your observations up the channel to your Oversoul. If there is anything that you need to know, ask your Oversoul to point it out to you.

Although in the beginning the process may feel cumbersome and awkward, it eventually will become spontaneous. In comparison, when you were a child learning to eat, using a knife, fork, and spoon felt equally cumbersome and awkward. It took concentration and practice to use those tools and get the food into your mouth, not all over your face. As an adult, you use those same utensils effortlessly. By the same token, as you practice the tools of communication just outlined, the more natural and effortless the process becomes.

You Only Communicate With Your Own Oversoul

You only communicate with your own Oversoul, and never with any other Oversoul. Whenever necessary, your Oversoul communicates with other Oversouls. Because all communication is filtered through one source, this method is very clean. Any information that you receive from your outer or inner worlds is always interpreted for your special needs.

Your Oversoul has complete knowledge of everything that you **need** to know, and communicates it back to you. This may be entirely different from what you **want** to know.

Explaining the outer world to you is the responsibility of your Oversoul. Collecting the data, passing it up, and interpreting the response are your responsibilities.

You Do Not Control

Through this method of communication, you do not control anyone. You only discuss something with your own Oversoul. It does the work for you.

For instance, you may decide to set up some experiments to determine if there is anything to this method of communication. You talk to your brother via the involved Oversouls, and he phones you to discuss exactly what you shared with him on the inner levels. You label this an interesting coincidence, and repeat the same experiment with a friend. Meeting him on the street, he also brings up the same things that you shared with him on the inner levels.

After several such incidents, you may begin to feel that **you** have the power to influence and control people. This is simply not so. It is your Oversoul that sets up the circumstances. If you take the credit instead of thanking your Oversoul for its help, these principles will stop working for you. Part of the responsibility for using these principles is recognizing that you alone have little power.

You can always tell your Oversoul what you do or do not want to happen. But because it has more knowledge, let it make the final decisions. Whatever your Oversoul allows to happen is always in your best interest. You may not always understand this, but as you objectively observe and ask questions, the reasons eventually become clear.

If you tell your Oversoul that you want a particular situation to occur regardless of the consequences, your Oversoul may allow it to happen so that you realize why it should not have happened.

Experiment On Your Own

Experiment on your own, and discover for yourself ways that your Oversoul can work with and for you. You are no longer alone. You are connecting with your true parent who wants to know you and your experiences.

Feelings

"Words are an essential form of communication, but as you move through them, you rediscover the importance of feeling."

When you were a baby, you did not understand words, yet you still understood what was happening around you. You understood feelings, and you communicated through feelings.

When the people around you were upset, you understood and you became upset. If they were laughing and happy, you laughed and were happy right along with them. You knew when they were just saying "No!" and when they really **meant** "No!"

At this stage in your life, you were totally in touch with your feelings. You knew when you were hungry and you let everyone know. You knew when you were uncomfortable and you let them know that, too. You were communicating in a language without words.

Replacing Feelings With Words

Eventually, as you learned to talk, you stopped identifying the feelings and began identifying the words. You **replaced** your knowledge of feelings with words, instead of **supplementing** your knowledge of feelings with words.

For example, as an adult you do not always know when you are hungry. You eat for entertainment, for pacifying depression, from boredom, or just because it is time. As an adult you often do not even use the correct words to describe what you feel.

You may use the words, "I am hungry," but what you really feel is, "I am bored. I would like some quick entertainment." You may even think that you are hungry.

You may use the words, "You make me angry," but what you really feel is frustration from a hard day at work. Not able to express your frustration during the day, you suppress that emotion. When you get home, you find yourself getting angry with your spouse or children. You think that they frustrate you. You have lost touch with the origin of your feelings.

Identify Your Feelings

Because you are accustomed to communicating with words, you have lost touch with much of your sense of feeling. The feelings still occur, but you do not take the time to identify them as feelings. Instead, you quickly move into the words that can only *try* to describe them.

All experience is feeling. Actually, feeling involves one or more of all five senses:

Taste—

Sweet and smooth are words that try to define what you feel when you eat.

Sight—

Barren and desolate are words that try to define what you feel when you see.

Hearing—

Pitch and rhythm are words that try to define what you feel when you listen.

Touch—

Soft and rough are words that try to define what you feel when you touch.

Smell—

Fresh and clean are words that try to define what you feel when you breathe.

Each of the five senses must be experienced to know what the words mean. You can use all the words that you want, yet you can only try to describe what an orange tastes like to a person who has never tasted one.

Tasting an orange is an experience that produces feelings inside of your mouth. Sweet, juicy, cool, and clean can only *try* to describe its taste. The other person may get a general idea, but never knows what it actually tastes like without the experience.

Life Without Words

If there were no words to help define your outer world, you would still develop a way to communicate with yourself.

For instance, every time you touched something soft, you would remember the feeling. Every time that you touched something rough, you would remember *that* feeling. You would identify a sameness of all soft objects, and a sameness of all rough objects.

Eventually, you would recognize the differences between rough and soft by identifying the feelings you experienced each time you touched one or the other. Even without words, you would still communicate with yourself.

You almost always express yourself with words. Even when no one is around, you think in words. Now, you must go backwards through your words to touch into your feeling nature.

You Unconsciously React

You already feel many things without stopping to identify them. Unconsciously, you react to these feelings without allowing this information to filter through into your conscious mind.

For example, when you walk into any room in your home you are unconsciously aware of many details. When you walk into your living room you know who the people in your family are without stopping to consciously identify them. Every object in that room has a story behind it. You know that story without stopping to consciously think about it. Each story is an experience, and each story produces different feelings.

Your best friend gave you a plant for your birthday and glancing at it makes you feel pleasant. Your favorite aunt gave you one of her most treasured knick-knacks which does not fit your decor. Because she comes to visit often, you must keep it on display. You try to avoid looking at it. But, both the plant and the knick-knack add to the atmosphere, or feeling, of the room.

Did you spend a wonderful evening last night with someone close? That feeling is still in the room when you walk in. Is there a fire in the fireplace? Colors, windows, books, stereos, paintings, and furniture all add to the feeling of the room.

Just by walking into your living room, you know all of this information in a split second by feeling it. Direct awareness gives you the knowledge. You know by knowing.

Slow Down

On some level of awareness you react to all the feelings that your outer world sends out. When you slow down long enough to feel these feelings, you can understand your reactions to any given situation.

For example, you have an important business meeting to attend. When you walk into the room, what feeling is projected in the room? Every place of business has its own feeling and usually reflects the personalities of the upper management. Is the room open and receptive? Does it have barriers? Is it cold? Just by walking into the room, you begin understanding the people with whom you will be doing business.

When you meet the people, what feelings do they project? Are they smiling and saying pleasant words, even though you feel anger and hostility in their auras? Is their anger and hostility directed at you? Or, is it at their supervisor, or family? And, are they directing those feelings at you because they need to clean out their anger? If so, how can you prepare yourself?

Their body language, clothing, and colors tell you who and what they are. These are reflections of their inner feelings.

Every person and object projects feelings. Slowing down allows you to feel whatever it is that your outer world projects. These feelings take you through illusion into the reality of what is. This allows you to accurately interpret any given situation, and respond accordingly.

Understanding the feelings of your outer world helps you to understand the feelings of your inner world. Through direct awareness you learn that one always complements the other.

Clean Up Your Words

Observe your words to determine when they match what you feel inside and when they do not. If you are bored, do not say that you are hungry, say that you are bored. You confuse people when you say that you are hungry but really you are bored.

They hear your words, but on some level they feel their double meaning. Because they do not know how to label what they feel, they become uncomfortable.

When your words match what you feel, you are touching into your feeling nature. This is called "cleaning up your words." People respond to the clarity of your words, and become more comfortable with you.

Cleaning up your words changes the reactions of other people to you. When you go home and state to your family, "I had a terribly frustrating day at work, and I feel frustrated!" you suddenly find the support that you have wanted for so many years. They react to the clarity of your words, and drop their defenses because they are no longer under attack. This teaches you to match feelings with feelings, and feelings with words.

Match Feelings With Feelings

As a child you were already matching feelings with feelings, but you lost much of that skill. For example, you may have wanted milk to drink. Your desire for milk is a feeling (taste). Instead of milk, you said water, so that is what you were given. You immediately identified the taste as something other than milk.

Your memory of the milk taste did not match the water taste. You had to wait until someone gave you milk and repeated the word again. You had to match that taste with the memory of your taste with the word being spoken. Then, you had to remember the word "milk" so that you could ask for it the next time.

This process is extremely painstaking for a child, and consumes a lot of time and energy. Because you thought it was no longer necessary, you have forgotten this process of trial and error.

Getting back in touch with your feelings is an interesting challenge. You may have to reach into some areas of your life that you are avoiding. You may feel uncomfortable, but that is okay. It is all part of the process. Remember, you already have the skill—it is just a bit rusty.

Your Oversoul Communicates Through Feeling

Your Oversoul communicates with you through feeling. You may receive pictures, symbols, sounds, words, and vibrations, but behind all of them is feeling. They direct your attention, but the knowing occurs when you accurately interpret the feeling behind them.

Using The Process Explains The Process

Many feelings are already coming forward from your inner world. Your willingness to acknowledge yourself automatically allows more information to surface into your conscious mind. This information comes in the form of feeling. Understanding the feeling tells you who you are.

Just as in meditation, using the process explains the process. For example, during meditation you receive a picture of a woman on a covered wagon. When you are in touch with your feelings, you automatically know the meaning of this picture. There is a process that teaches you to understand the meaning of the picture within seconds.

Project your consciousness up into the channel that connects you to your Oversoul. Feel if the woman in the picture feels like you. If she does, then you are seeing yourself in another lifeline. In the same way, you communicate with your Oversoul by asking questions and feeling the answers.

Through the process of trial and error, ask a question and feel an answer. If the feelings match, you have your answer. If not, continue asking questions until they do. For example:

What does the woman on the covered wagon feel?

Is she exuberant and excited?
    When you know what exuberance and excitement feel like, you know by knowing the answer.

Is she exhausted and weary?
    When you know what exhaustion and weariness feel like, you know by knowing the answer.

Is she married?
 What does being married feel like?
 What does being single feel like?
 Which feeling matches the way she feels?

Continue to ask questions and match feelings until you know everything that you need to know about her—

How old she is:
    Does she feel like—

a teenager?
a middle-aged person?
an older person?
someone in her thirties? forties?

Where she came from:
  Does she feel like she came from—
    the East Coast?
    the Midwest?
    England?

If she had any children, and if so, how many:
  What does it feel like—
    not to have any children?
    to have one child? two children? six children? boys? girls? boys and girls?

If she was happy—
  What does feeling happy feel like?
  What does feeling unhappy feel like?

If she completed the trip, and why or why not—
  What does it feel like to complete a trip?
  What does it feel like not to complete a trip?

How long she lived—
  Can you feel her at thirty, but not at forty?

Continue to ask questions and match feelings. You can determine whatever your Oversoul wants you to know by understanding the feeling that is behind one picture. You "know by knowing" so many things from one picture, the same as you "know by knowing" when you walk into your living room.

Daily Guidance

In the same way, ask for daily guidance from your Oversoul. Continue the process of matching feelings, utilizing the clues to direct your learning. As an example, you decide to discuss something important with a friend and you are not sure if you should approach him/her now, or wait.

First, ask your Oversoul if the timing is correct.

Project your consciousness up into the channel that connects with your Oversoul.

From past experience, remember what correct timing feels like—
The person reacted favorably.
The conversation went smoothly.
You felt satisfied that you were heard.
(This set of experiences left a feeling inside of you).

From past experience, remember what incorrect timing feels like—
The person acted put out.

The conversation was awkward.
You knew that your time was wasted.
(This set of experiences left a feeling inside of you).

What are you feeling in the channel?
Does it match the feelings that correct timing produces?
Does it match the feelings that incorrect timing produces?

You think it matches the feelings that correct timing produces, so you decide to speak to your friend now.

After speaking to your friend, you evaluate—
Did the person react favorably?
Did the conversation go smoothly?
Were you satisfied that you were heard?

If you answer yes to the above questions, then you correctly interpreted the communication from your Oversoul. Remember this feeling so that you can repeat the experience and go through the steps faster.

If you answer no to the above questions, then you have direct knowledge of what it is like when you do not correctly interpret the communication from your Oversoul. It is just as important to know when you do not correctly interpret the communication from your Oversoul. This allows you to build a data base of both types of feelings.

You Have A Partner

What your Oversoul directs you to do may not always coincide with what you want. Your Oversoul is your partner, and because it is the one with the most knowledge, it always has the final say.

For example, you may want to gossip about someone, but your Oversoul directs you not to. If you gossip anyway, the power of your words will return to you with the same force that you sent them. Because you have more knowledge, you must balance your actions with wisdom. In other words, you are now more accountable for your actions.

You may want to spend your money one way, but your Oversoul tells you to spend it another way. You may want to dress for an occasion one way, and your Oversoul may direct you into different clothing.

The more that you work with your inner guidance, the easier it becomes to interpret it. As you learn to interpret it, you learn to trust it. What you previously labeled "hunches" takes on new meaning.

Next, you may go through a period where you want to listen to your Oversoul, but you do not. This is because you may be told something that you do not want to hear.

When you pass through that stage, you listen, but do as you want anyway. During this time, you learn that had you listened in the first place, you would have been happier with the outcome. You may not always know why your Oversoul directs you, but if you observe and pay attention, the reasons eventually become clearer.

Move Upward Into Your Potential

This rebellion is normal. You are unaccustomed to this type of guidance. You are used to acting independently, even if you chose to give that independence to another person. You now give your independence to your Oversoul, knowing that it helps you to quickly grow by pulling you upward into your potential.

Know By Knowing

The more you practice interpreting feelings, the more adept you become at understanding them. You know by knowing what you feel, what feelings other people and objects project, and what your Oversoul communicates to you.

You recognize and interpret a sizable amount of information in a split second, just by feeling. You know so much that it takes longer to articulate all that you know than it does to feel it. This is the same process that you go through every day when you walk into your living room.

All you have to do is recognize what you are already doing, label it, and then take the time to consciously repeat the experience at will. Whenever you understand feelings, you know by knowing. It is within this level that you have direct awareness.

The deeper that you touch into your feeling nature, the more you understand. Words are an essential form of communication, but as you move through them, you rediscover the importance of feeling.

RELEASING THE PAST

*"Because you no longer react as intensely through your past experiences,
it becomes easier to focus on the present moment."*

Every day brings new experiences into your life. Each experience teaches you something, whether you are aware of it or not. If you do not learn from an experience, you continue to have similar experiences until you learn whatever it is that you need to know.

All experiences have an effect upon you, whether you recognize this or not. After the experience is gone, the feeling of the experience remains with you. This feeling is vibration, and leaves an imprint in your personal energy field, or aura.

Your Aura Reflects Your Experiences

Your aura reflects your experiences through:

Color

Clarity

Symbols

Patterns

Flow

Smell

Rate of vibration

Vibratory Imprints Are Cumulative

You are individualized neutral energy with the vibrations of your experiences circulating around you. As similar experiences are repeated, the feelings that are left are drawn to the "like" vibratory imprints that already exist within your aura and strengthen them. These vibratory imprints are cumulative—not only in this lifetime, but from one to another, and affect your mental and emotional state.

Every time you are angry, the experience leaves a feeling within you. These feelings pass into your body, then out into your aura. They are attracted to like vibratory imprints. Illusion tells you that the anger experience is over, but reality tells you that it is only out of your conscious mind.

On some level of awareness, you still feel and react to that anger experience, as well as to the cumulative ones that surround you. The more anger experiences you have, the stronger the vibratory imprint for anger becomes.

You react to your everyday experiences through these accumulated vibratory imprints. Because you react through them, any situation can easily make you angry. For example, one of your children accidentally breaks a piece of your good china. It becomes an excuse to vent some of your accumulated anger. Then, you wonder why you got so angry, and you feel guilty. Because you have so much suppressed anger buried in your body and aura, you need some way to release it. This usually means that you try to clean out your pain by inflicting it on someone else.

Vibratory Imprints Affect the Body

Feelings create vibratory imprints. When vibratory imprints grow strong enough, they directly affect the physical body. They are something that can be seen and felt on some level of awareness. You actually manifest something, the same as you do when you put a bubble around your aura.

As they grow stronger, they become more dense and settle into your physical body. This effect can either be positive or negative, and you actually wear these vibratory imprints in your body. These vibratory imprints affect:

Your quality of health—
  How well your body functions on a daily basis.
  Any chronic illness.

Mannerisms—
  How you talk, walk, gesture, carry yourself.

Tension—
  If it is or is not present in your body; if so, where.

Your body is affected by all of the feelings that you have ever had.

Releasing Vibratory Imprints

Your aura and physical body can only contain a given number of vibratory imprints. Eventually, they become full, and the vibratory imprints must be released. There are five ways to release them:

Accidents

Illness

Words

Physical death

Consciously to your Oversoul

Accidents

The established vibratory imprints that surround you can become so thick and heavy that they must have some type of physical impact to release them. An accident quickly creates the impact that you need. It can be a major one, or perhaps only a bump on the head. An accident releases the patterns by breaking them up and dispersing them before they become so dense that they create a major illness in your body.

Illness

Illness rearranges the vibratory imprints that surround you. Fevers burn up and clean out vibratory imprints that are becoming dense. This releases them before they turn into a chronic illness. A chronic illness is the result of specific repeated negative behavior patterns.

Sometimes when you are working very hard to make changes, you may cause a minor illness because you are releasing the toxins that negative feelings have left behind. You feel their effects on their way out of your body.

Because body, mind, and spirit are all interconnected, it does not matter which spoke on the wheel gets rearranged. One always directly affects the other. Rearranging the biological structure of the body through illness changes something in your mental, emotional, and/or spiritual bodies.

Words

Words provide a quick and easy release for your vibratory imprints. When an especially happy or upsetting event occurs, for instance, you cannot wait to tell someone about it. Your thoughts are energy, and speaking them releases some of this energy. You feel it go.

This is especially easy to demonstrate when you are angry. You feel the anger well up in your solar plexus, or stomach area. You feel it come right up your throat and out of your mouth. When you are through speaking, you feel drained.

You have cleaned yourself out. Unfortunately, you have only put those anger feelings out into the air. Because they are a part of you, they eventually come back to you. Anger going out means anger coming back.

Physical Death

Eventually, even with accidents, illness, and spoken words, your aura and body become full. Your body dies, and you go directly to your Oversoul to release the vibratory imprints of your accumulated past experiences if your Oversoul wants them. Together, you review your life: what you learned and what still needs to be learned. You decide which experiences are completed and which ones are not. Your Oversoul may take all of your experiences, some of them, or none of them.

Conscious Release

The last way to clean out vibratory imprints is to consciously release them up to your Oversoul. When you consciously release them, you do not have to carry the feelings that they have left within and around you. Releasing negative patterns means that you no longer have to wear them in your body or aura.

It is also important to release positive vibratory imprints, because they too are the result of leftover feelings from past experiences. You need the space around you as clear and clean as possible.

Your Aura And Body Reflect Your Work

As you release in conscious awareness, your aura and body reflect the work that you are doing.
Your aura—

Changes color.

Becomes clearer.

Becomes less dense.

Changes symbols and patterns.

Smells cleaner.

Flows smoother and more evenly.

Quickens its rate of vibration.

Your physical body—

Looks younger.

Functions more efficiently on a daily basis.

Releases its tension.

Changes its mannerisms.

Begins healing any chronic illness.

Cleaning Yourself Up

You might compare yourself to a child that has never had a bath. It is possible to wash away the dirt that has accumulated not only in this lifetime, but also in others. Consciously releasing vibratory imprints allows you to remove the feelings that past experiences have left in your body and aura that are no longer necessary.

This cleaning process allows you to evaluate your life more clearly. You no longer have to view it through the feelings of past experiences. Because you are less agitated by vibratory imprints that are not calm and peaceful, you automatically become calmer and more peaceful.

It becomes easier to walk through the turmoil of the outer world without being pulled into it. While remaining centered and balanced, you can objectively observe whatever is happening around you. With less agitation to pull you outward, you also will find it easier to go into deeper levels of inner awareness during meditation.

Release Daily Experiences

To keep vibratory imprints from accumulating, release daily experiences to your Oversoul as they occur. This releasing process allows you to review your daily activities, and evaluate:

What you learned.

What still needs to be learned.

How you can learn it.

With the permission and guidance of your Oversoul, make changes in your life moment by moment, day by day. Become a conscious partner in your personal development and spiritual growth.

Pleasant Experiences

Releasing daily activities is not always as easy as it sounds, and is a skill that must be developed. It does not matter if the experience is positive or negative. You may not want to let go of pleasant experiences because you think that they are too far and few between. You may want to hold onto them until you are certain that you will have another one.

Conflict

Surprisingly, you even want to hold onto conflict. Conflict has always played an important role and has been a wonderful teacher and entertainer. If you release known events, you must replace them with unknown events. Replacing conflict with an unknown can be very scary.

After eons of learning through conflict, there may be a part of you that does not want to give it up. This part has worked long and hard through many lifetimes to gain experience from that conflict. Explain to that part of yourself that you appreciate its knowledge, but your Oversoul needs the information that it contains. Tell it that if you need to contact it, you will do so through your Oversoul.

The Past

As you become competent in releasing daily activities, experiences and feelings from your past start coming forward into your conscious mind. Release everything up to your Oversoul, observing it as it passes out of you. Any experience that still causes a strong reaction from you is not finished.

Will yourself into your center, and let the part of you that still reacts complete that experience. Let it feel any emotion that it wants to, and express itself accordingly. Release those feelings up the channel to your Oversoul. When you are ready to totally release the experience, you can identify both the positive and negative aspects of it. You feel neutral toward the experience.

Sometimes your illusions may tell you that you feel neutral toward an experience. The reality may be that you are ignoring some negative aspects. Be sure to examine every corner of yourself. In order to clean yourself out, you must acknowledge what exists within you.

Simultaneous Y

As you cleanse yourself, experiences from simultaneous lives may also begin to come forward into your conscious mind. Release these on up to your Oversoul and ask for an explanation. Ask your Oversoul to explain why this particular life is being shown to you and what significance it has on your present.

If you do not receive an explanation, do not keep the experience but release it back up until you receive one. In order to move deeper into the level of knowing by knowing, you must release the level that teaches you to know by guessing. Trust that what you need to know will be explained when it has relevance to you.

Focus On The Present

Because you no longer react as intensely through your past experiences, it becomes easier to focus on the present moment. You react to the present, rather than to memories of past experiences. You have a better understanding of why you are doing what you are doing, when you are doing it. You learn from and appreciate the present moment.

Using The Process

Only by releasing everything to your Oversoul can you be cleansed. This process allows you to view your life from a more objective perspective. The more objective you can be, the more accurate your evaluations. Then you can identify specific patterns of behavior, and make conscious decisions on what and how to change.

The releasing process continues to build your connections with universal energy. It moves your energy up and down, and strengthens your communication with your Oversoul. As you use the process, you learn about the process. And, the process continues to teach you through direct awareness.

GROWING YOUNGER

*"Your body is a product of your own thoughts and is proof
of the power you hold."*

People age at an artificially accelerated rate. On some level of awareness people automatically assume that they will grow old, and deteriorate mentally and physically. The collective unconscious tells them that they will grow old and deteriorate.

Many people exercise and watch their diet, but there is one more factor to maintaining youth. The physical body is also a creation of vibratory imprints.

The Body Is A Parable

The physical body is a reflection of past experiences. For example, you can interpret the lifetime experiences of people by observing them. Their faces may be smiling, but the lines on them, the roundness of shoulders, and the heaviness of walk all tell in parable the stories of their lives.

Their bodies tell you that life has not always been easy, and that they have struggled through pain and conflict. They can also tell you specific experiences and feelings. Their bodies carry the weight of their vibratory imprints.

Because these vibratory imprints are cumulative, often by the time people are in their twenties, their bodies already show signs of aging. Their mannerisms and facial expressions reflect the struggles of childhood and early adult years. They may have a little extra weight, which reflects the extra mental baggage, or vibratory imprints, that they carry with them. Or, they may look rigid and tense from the density of their vibratory imprints.

As each decade rolls by and more vibratory imprints accumulate, the aging process speeds up. Your body continues to be a parable that tells you and others about your past experiences. You carry all of the leftover feelings of your past experiences with you, and it can be a heavy burden.

You Do Not Have To Carry The Weight Of Your Past

It is possible to have the knowledge of your past actions without carrying the effects of their vibratory imprints with you. You can release your feelings from your experiences, as they occur, up to your Oversoul. This releases them from your aura and keeps it clear and clean. Your body does not have to reflect your life experiences. You do not have to carry the weight of your past with you.

Your Oversoul is waiting for your experiences. It wants to know:

What you experienced.

How you reacted.

How other people reacted.

What emotions you felt.

Rather than wait to tell your Oversoul at the end of your life, consciously release all of that information now.

Visualize Your Oversoul As A Sun

Your Oversoul is neutral energy. Because at this point you do not know exactly what this energy looks like, or even if you have an Oversoul, experiment with some of the following principles to determine their validity.

Visualize your Oversoul as a bright sun above your head, connected by a clear, elasticized channel. To release your experiences, send your thoughts, feelings, and pictures up this channel. Watch them disappear into the sun, observing that the sun always stays clean.

Release Your Feelings

Release all of the feelings from your experiences at the end of each day. Trying to hold onto them may cause sleeplessness. In some instances negative feelings can keep you awake by providing hours of entertainment. Holding onto positive feelings helps prolong positive experiences.

The feelings from daily experiences settle into the physical body fairly quickly. A cramp in your leg at night, for example, reminds you of the fun that you had on a hike. A headache reminds you of the tension of the day. Both are examples of how quickly vibratory imprints settle into the body.

Take a few minutes each morning to release your learning from the night. All kinds of learning occur while you sleep. On some level of awareness your night learning also produces feelings that accumulate in your aura.

Keep Cleaning

The most efficient way to keep yourself clean is to release the feelings of any experience as it occurs. All you have to do is feel and/or watch your feelings pass up the channel to your Oversoul.

If you forget to release them, ask your Oversoul to clean up your leftover feelings from the past week, month, year, or years. Feel and watch them leave your body and aura en masse.

You do not have to go into a meditative state to clean. Start right now by stopping for a couple of minutes, and will the cleaning to begin. Clean yourself up anytime you happen to think about it—while watching television, doing laundry, driving, or even exercising.

Cleaning actually releases something from yourself. These leftover feelings which comprise your vibratory imprints are a creation of your thoughts, and have weight. They are dark and heavy, and usually muddy brown or black. Watch them go up the channel, and feel how much lighter and cleaner you are.

Continue cleaning any time that you happen to think about it. Because your vibratory imprints have accumulated over a long period of time, you most likely will not release them all at once. It takes time to effectively clean yourself out.

Strong Vibratory Imprints

When you have had many, many similar experiences, the vibratory imprints that result from them are very strong. Some are so strong, they almost seem to have a will of their own. No matter how many times you try to release them up to your Oversoul, they never seem to weaken. These vibratory imprints have been fed very well from your leftover feelings. In a sense, they have become a type of life form. They are a part of you, yet separate from you.

Now, all of a sudden, you are telling your creation to remove itself from your life. Naturally, it does not want to leave and it is going to protest. Releasing it from your space means that it must venture into the unknown and it does not want to go. It thinks that you are trying to destroy it and it tries to hang on harder.

Call up this part of yourself, either during meditation, or whenever you have a quiet moment to yourself. Visualize it as an image of yourself talking to the you that is in your center. Ask this image why it does not want to go. Allow it to talk and talk until it is out of words and is exhausted.

Thank it for sharing itself and explain that it is important. You appreciate it and all that it has gone through to acquire its knowledge. However, your Oversoul now wants it. Whenever you need any information that it has, you will communicate with it through your Oversoul.

Visualize yourself handing this part of you up through the channel and into the cloud that represents your Oversoul. If it comes back, repeat this procedure. Continue to hand it back to your Oversoul.

Working With Negative Emotions

This method is especially useful when working with negative emotions. For instance, if you want to remove the vibratory imprint of anger from your aura, you are going to discover that many experiences have contributed to that imprint.

When you release it up, it may keep returning. Visualize this angry part of yourself, and ask it why it is angry. Allow it to tell you, while you stay in your center as the objective observer. When it is through, thank it, and release it up to your Oversoul.

Removing Blocks

This method is helpful for removing blocks of any kind. Say you do not like to balance your checkbook, but you want to start balancing it. Call up the part of you that does not like this activity, and ask it to explain why. Let it talk, do not try to suppress it, and listen. You may be surprised at what it tells you. Seemingly unrelated events may surface that you had forgotten about long ago. These events can be cleaned up by releasing them, and you can finally keep your checkbook balanced.

Positive And Negative Aspects

When a vibratory imprint is finally weakened enough to move completely out of your aura, you will be aware of both the positive and negative aspects of the experiences that have produced your feelings. For example, you will know all of the positive and negative aspects of not keeping your checkbook balanced.

Some of the positive aspects are:
You do not have to worry about the amount of money in your checking account since you do not know how much it is.
You provide another reason to argue with your spouse, allowing you to clean out pent-up frustrations.
You have more time for things that you really enjoy.

Some of the negative aspects are:
Because you do not know how much money you have, you do not know how much you can spend.
You wish you did not have so many arguments with your spouse so that you could feel closer.
You feel guilty when you do not have an accurate checkbook balance, because with a little effort, you know that you could.

Releasing Excess Aura Weight

Not all vibratory imprints can be released at once. But, you can begin to break them up and release them from your aura. You feel calmer and more peaceful as you release this excess baggage. The weight released from your aura will be reflected in your body, regardless of your chronological years.

If you have ever gained and lost weight, it is much the same feeling. You can easily put on ten pounds without realizing that you have gained any weight. Have you ever looked at a ten-pound sack of flour in the grocery store and wondered what it would be like to have it strapped to your back all day? It would be quite a weight to carry.

So, how could you put on ten pounds and not notice it? It is not until you actually take off those ten pounds that you realize how sluggish you felt with the extra weight. It is the same with your accumulated vibratory imprints. You do not realize their weight and effects until you take them off, or in this case, release them up to your Oversoul.

Keep Yourself Strong And Solid

Not only do you carry the leftover feelings of your experiences, but you have scattered your feelings all around you. The impact from the accidents that you have had, the words that you have spoken, material objects that you have created and/or touched, and even your thoughts, have dispersed your vibratory imprints from your aura. You want your feelings gathered in one place to keep you as strong and solid as possible.

Ask your Oversoul to pull all your feelings in from any place that you have been during the day. If you do not, then other people will react to the thoughts and feelings that you have left behind. Visualize a giant vacuum cleaner sucking up all of the vibrations that you left, and then watch them disappear into the sun that is your Oversoul.

Do Not Scatter Yourself

Once your vibratory imprints have been pulled into your Oversoul, do your best to keep from scattering yourself. You can ask that your feelings be cleaned up and released to your Oversoul on an event-by-event basis, or daily, weekly, or even yearly. However, the sooner that you get pulled back into yourself, the stronger and more solid you will be.

Distinguish What Is Yours

The releasing process teaches you through direct awareness that there are many areas in your life which you think are yours and yours alone, but which are not. Just as you have scattered your feelings wherever you have been, other people have also scattered themselves around you. Why deal with their feelings and frustrations when you have enough of your own?

For example, not all of the feelings in your home are yours. You not only react through the accumulated feelings of your past experiences, you also react to the thoughts and feelings that other people have unconsciously dumped in your home.

On some level, you react to the feelings that previous owners and their guests have left. You react to the feelings of the people who manufactured the furniture in your home and who produced the food in your refrigerator. Every time someone touches something, they leave a bit of themselves behind.

The reason that mom's home cooking tastes so good, for example, is not always because she is such a wonderful cook. Not only do you eat the food that she has prepared, you also ingest the feelings behind the food. You feel the time and care that she spent planning, purchasing, and preparing it. She not only nourishes you with the food that you see with your physical eyes, she also nourishes you with her care.

But, when you ingest her care, you also ingest whatever feelings she attaches to her care. It may be a concern for you, a fear that you are not happy, or a frustration that she cannot do more for you. You do not want those feelings in you.

For this reason it is important to distinguish what is yours and what is not. Ask your Oversoul to bless the food and release any feelings that are not yours. Ask that those feelings be cleaned up and returned to their rightful owner. Your Oversoul will take care of the logistics. This continues to keep you clean and clear.

Clean Up As Much As Possible

Cleaning up as many experiences as possible means that you only deal with yourself. Allow other people to have what is rightfully theirs and keep only what is yours. You cannot mix others' feelings with yours if you want to find out who you are.

The following is a list to help you get started with the cleaning process:

Conversations—
  Ask that the energy of your words be cleaned up and returned to your Oversoul.
  Ask that any misunderstandings be clarified through the involved Oversouls.

Relationships—

  Ask that they be cleaned up, explained, and the knowledge returned to you.

Health—
  Ask that your body be cleaned up and strengthened so that it can provide the most efficient home for you while you are here.

Finances—
  Ask that your feelings be released from any money that you spend.
  Give thanks that it has been provided for you, and let go of it with appreciation.

Home—
  Ask that any feelings in your home that do not belong to you be cleaned up and returned to their   rightful owners.
  When you have had visitors, ask that their feelings be cleaned up and returned to them.

Possessions—
  All of your possessions have been handled by many people who have all left some of their feelings on them.
  Ask that they be cleaned up, and any feelings that are not yours be returned to their rightful owners.

Food—
  Ask that any food that you eat be blessed, cleaned up, and the feelings of others be returned to their rightful owners.

Bodily waste—
  It also contains your vibrations. Ask that your vibrations be returned to your Oversoul, and the physical waste continue on its journey.

Anything that you give away or sell—
Ask that your vibrations be returned to your Oversoul.
Ask that it be cleaned up and made ready for its new owner, whomever that might be.

When you stop and put labels on all the feelings that you carry with you, you understand why your body ages so quickly.

Your Psychic Energy

Cleaning yourself up and releasing the excess weight of vibratory imprints allows your personal, or psychic energy to flow with less constraints.

With age, the psychic energy slows down because it must constantly push through all of the accumulated vibratory imprints that have settled into the body. For example, your body cannot always effectively use the food that you feed it because the psychic energy which controls the digestive enzymes gets bogged down with the weight of your vibratory imprints.

The entire system is thrown out of balance when the energy that has been provided for it cannot be fully utilized. As unnecessary vibratory imprints are released, psychic energy flows more freely through the body. It can do what it needs to do, and as a result, the body functions much more efficiently.

Slowing Down The Aging Process

You can slow down the aging process by taking a few minutes every day to release some of your leftover feelings. Your chronological age does not matter. Cleaning out your vibratory imprints lightens your aura and pulls an amazing amount of weight off of your physical body.

One day, you will look in the mirror, and realize that you do look younger and more vibrant. Your skin has better color and your face and body look more relaxed. This encourages you to continue releasing, which in turn allows you to build a stronger, healthier body, regardless of your chronological age.

Love Your Body

When you look at your body in the mirror, take a moment to love it. Realize that you created whatever it is that your body is expressing. Instead of ignoring, chastising, or criticizing the parts that you do not like, or do not think work the way that they "should", tell them that you love them.

Remember, your body is a product of your own thoughts, and is proof of the power that you hold. What you do with that power is always your choice. It is your decision whether you use it to tear your body down or to build a strong and healthy one.

You Are Limitless

"Through direct awareness, you know by knowing that you are
infinitely deep, with an infinite well of answers."

You are discovering that all of your answers are within and around you. You are recognizing and utilizing the clues that take you into these answers. Using your answers, you are moving into continually deeper levels of inner awareness.

You are finding out how much you already know. All you are doing differently is slowing yourself down long enough to recognize what you know. Then, you are labeling and defining it so that you can repeat the process at will.

Your Reactions Are Changing

Your inner and outer worlds are the same as before you started this book, but now you are viewing them from a different perspective. This changes your reaction to them, and, in turn, their reaction to you.

Activating Inner Healing

Being aware of who and what you are automatically activates your inner healing process. Through direct awareness, you "know by knowing" that you can:

Find your own answers.

Define yourself.

Accept who you are.

Like who you are.

Clean up your past.

Take responsibility for yourself and your life.

Lay out the patterns for your future.

Make a difference in your inner and outer worlds.

Define spirituality and God-Mind.

Validate Your Information

This book is a catalyst to move you into deeper levels of inner awareness. It is only a beginning point to give you direction. This book does not do the work, or give you experience. It is up to you to validate the information and to determine what works and what does not.

There are many avenues of action, and just as many interpretations of those avenues. Always validate knowledge for yourself. Never be satisfied to say:

I read it in a book, so it must be true.

Someone told me, so it must be true.

You are becoming a scientist who gathers data, experiments with it, asks questions, and continually reevaluates it until you can say:

I know through direct awareness.

I know because I experienced it; this is what did or did not happen.

I know by knowing.

Being aware of the tools that can take you into the knowledge is a beginning point. But, only when you have used them to gather your own data and applied it, is that knowledge truly yours. When you understand what you have learned by experiencing and feeling it, then you can say, "I know by knowing".

Be Open And Honest

Always ask your Oversoul and God-Mind to direct your learning. Be willing to move into deeper levels of inner awareness. This can only be accomplished when you are open and honest with yourself.

Grow Step By Step

Allow your life to grow in an orderly manner, step by step. Once you learn how to use one set of tools, the doors will open a little wider. Another set of tools will be waiting to take you into even deeper levels of inner awareness.

Through direct awareness, you know by knowing that you are infinitely deep, with an infinite well of answers. You already had the knowledge, and now you have some tools to help you access that knowledge.

Always be willing to move; to be open and receptive to growth and change. Never set limits for yourself; you might reach them and stay there. Set goals, and use them as significant events, continuing to recognize that you truly are limitless.

APPENDICES I

SOME THINGS TO TRY

RING ON A STRING I

Demonstrate the power of your mind—
Attach a piece of string to a ring.
Hold the string between your thumb and forefingers.
Steady your arm.
With your thoughts, will the ring to move in a circle.
Allow a few seconds for this to happen.

Once it does, you can will it to—
Move in larger or smaller circles.
Change directions.
Go back and forth.

RING ON A STRING II

Keep your arm steady—
Hold the ring above someone else's head, in the space that contains his/her thoughts.
Ask him/her to will the ring to move.
Observe what happens.

Try this—
Above a woman's head.
Above a man's head.
Observe the difference

ABUNDANCE

Allow yourself to feel abundance—

Visualize all that you desire flowing in and through you, for example, positive relationships, health, finances, career, patience, etc.

Give thanks to your Oversoul for opening the universal flow.

CREATE A BUBBLE

Using the power of your thoughts, pull your aura in close to your body. Create a violet bubble around it by taking a second or two to visualize one there.

You can make it as thick as you want to.

Evaluate your feelings—
   Are you less tired around groups of people with it than without it?
   Does it affect your ability to communicate?

ALL EXPERIENCES TEACH

Think of an experience that causes you pain, misery, suffering, and/or discomfort: List the perks.
   List the growth that it has brought you:

What did it teach you about your own capabilities—
   Your strengths; weaknesses; potential?

What did it teach you about other people?

FEEL THE SAMENESS AND DIFFERENCES

Practice feeling and identifying the feelings of sameness and differences:

Feel the sameness of all—
     Schools
     Hospitals
     Grocery stores
     Government agencies
     Funeral homes

Once you can feel the sameness of each group, then feel the differences between each group.

FEEL YOUR HOME

Your home has a unique feeling. Feel how your home feels different
from anyone else's home:

Stop and feel the colors that you have chosen—
  How do they make you feel?
  How are they reflective of your personality?
Are they:
  bright and cheery?
  warm and cozy?
  soft and peaceful?
  cold and hard?
  dark and gloomy?

What feeling does your furniture project?

How do you feel about the windows and lighting in your home?

Does your home feel cluttered?

Does your home feel like you?

Does your home feel like your family?

Does one room feel more like one person than another?

What feelings do your personal belongings project?

How do you feel when you hold specific objects?

Do you have things in your home that you do not particularly like?
If so, why do you keep them? Is it time to clean them out?

Continue asking questions that allow you to feel your home.

FEEL YOUR BODY

Is it possible that your body is full of leftover feelings from past experiences
that you no longer need? How would it feel if it did not contain leftover feelings?

FEEL ADVERTISEMENTS

When reading a newspaper or magazine, stop and feel the
differences that each ad projects.
Each ad contains the feeling of the company that it came from.
Ask yourself the following questions as you feel the ads:

What does the ad convey about the feeling of the company?
Is it a company that you would want to do business with?
Why do you choose one company over another?
Do the ads of similar businesses have similar feelings?

SPEAK THROUGH YOUR OVERSOUL

Before you speak to anyone, address that person first through your Oversoul:

Explain what you want to talk about and why—

When you do talk to him/her, observe if he/she is any more receptive than usual.

Notice if that person brings up any of your concerns before you do.

Think of a situation or person that you are avoiding: Talk to the involved persons
through your Oversoul. Verbally speak to those persons. Observe their reaction: Do you
think it is any different than if you had not prepared them through your Oversoul?

Collect your data:

Observe when you think that communicating through your Oversoul makes a
difference and when you do not.

AFFIRMATIONS

The following affirmations are short, simple, and easy to use. Choose one or two to think or say throughout your day. You might even like to write them. Expand or change them any way that personalizes them for you.

ACCEPTING YOUR BODY

I accept and appreciate my body.
I ask my Oversoul and God-Mind to bless my body.
I give thanks for my body.
I love my body.
I love (any part of your body that you don't like).
I love (any part of your body that doesn't work the way
you think it "should").

ACCEPTING YOURSELF

I am willing to stop hiding from myself.
I accept my dual nature.
I learn from my positive and negative aspects and experiences.
I allow all experiences to teach me.
I am gentle with myself.
I accept my own self-worth.
I accept myself as I am.

APPRECIATION

I give thanks to my Oversoul and God-Mind for directing my inner learning.
I give thanks to my Oversoul and God-Mind for knowledge, and for the wisdom
to use it wisely.
I give thanks to my Oversoul and God-Mind for all that I have and all that I receive.

CONSCIOUS AWARENESS

I act in conscious awareness.
My energy flows vertically.
Whatever I need to know comes forward into my conscious mind.
I am able to find my own answers with the help of my Oversoul and God-Mind.

CONSCIOUS RELEASE

I consciously release my life to my Oversoul and God-Mind.
I release any feelings and experiences that I no longer need.
I am able to release my pleasant experiences.
I release my pleasant experiences to make room for more.
I am able to release my unpleasant experiences.
I no longer need to learn in a negative way.
I am willing to release my past.
I release any blocks that keep me from moving forward.

FEELINGS

I understand my feelings.
I identify the origin of my feelings.
I am able to accurately feel what I need to know.

INNER AWARENESS
I move into continually deeper levels of inner awareness.
I know by knowing.
I know through direct awareness.
I acknowledge and accept my limitlessness.

INNER HEALING
I am willing to grow step by step.
I am responsible for my own inner healing.
I activate my own inner healing.
I take responsibility for my life.
I ask my Oversoul and God-Mind to direct me in my inner healing.

MEDITATION
I am able to sit quietly.
I am able to go deep within my center.
I objectively observe myself without judgment or criticism.
I feel the oneness with All That Is.
I feel the expansion of myself beyond my body.
I feel the natural rhythm of the universe as it expands and contracts.
I learn through direct awareness.

PRESENT MOMENT
I slow down and learn from my present moment.
I enjoy my present moment.
My present moment teaches me about myself, my Oversoul, and God-Mind.

MEDITATIONS TO GET YOU STARTED

SITTING QUIETLY I

If sitting quietly is difficult for you, try the following for five minutes for a few days:

Gently bend and stretch to release any tension that is present in your body. Sit outside or at a window with your eyes open.

Observe your surroundings and think about the following questions—
 Do you enjoy what you are looking at?
 What things change from day to day?
 What things stay the same?
 Does the air have any particular feel or smell?
 What emotions do you feel?
 Do you enjoy spending five minutes just sitting?

Observe your body and think about these questions—
 Is it able to sit quietly for five minutes?
 Does it enjoy the time, or does it feel agitated?
 Is there tension in any part of it?
 What parts are more relaxed than other parts?

Do not criticize or judge your thoughts and feelings.

Merely observe what occurs within you and your body.

SITTING QUIETLY II

Once you can sit quietly with your eyes open, then try the following for five minutes for a few days:

Gently bend and stretch to release any tension that is present in your body.

Sit in a comfortable chair that allows your spine to be straight.

Place your feet flat on the floor.

Place your hands in your lap, palm up in a receptive position.

Close your eyes.

Observe the emotions that you feel, and ask yourself the following questions—
 Do I feel comfortable or uncomfortable? Do I feel calm inside?
 Do I enjoy sitting quietly?

Observe how your body feels, and ask yourself these questions—
Does it feel comfortable, or does it feel agitated?
Does it hold tension? If it does, release it by willing the muscles holding the tension to relax.
Does it enjoy sitting quietly?

Do not criticize or judge your thoughts and feelings.

Merely observe what occurs within you and your body.

MEDITATION PRAYER

If you feel comfortable doing so, begin and end your meditation time with a prayer.

For example, open your meditation time with the following statement:
I thank my Oversoul and God-Mind for preparing me for this meditation time.
I am receptive to all that you wish to teach me.

Close your meditation time with the following statement:
Thank you for all that I learned during my meditation time. I give thanks.

FEEL THE DIFFERENCES

During meditation, feel the differences in the substances that your breath passes through.

As you breathe in and out—
Feel your breath pass through your physical body.
Feel your breath move into the space above your head that contains your thoughts.
Feel how far this space extends outward and upward.
Feel its shape and density.

Then, going beyond these limits, feel your breath move into the channel that connects you to your Oversoul.
Feel the space inside your channel.
When you feel beneath your breath, feel the space that holds your thoughts.
When you feel above your breath, feel the channel that extends up to your Oversoul.
Feel how the space in your channel feels different from the space that contains your thoughts.
Remember that feeling so that you can move into the channel whenever you wish.
Release your feelings up to your Oversoul, and complete your meditation.

SECTION II
MOVING FORWARD

UNRAVELING THE MYSTERIES

*"Once you make a decision to grow vertically, you maybe surprised
at the acceleration of your growth rate."*

Imagine yourself the guest of honor at a party. There are five wrapped gifts on the table in front of you. Each one for you, but there is one catch. You can only open one gift every hour. Thus begins an evening of fun, intrigue, and, yes, mystery!

Opening the gifts over a period of time extends the excitement. The wait intensifies the entertainment. The anticipation of what is inside adds to the intrigue. Opening those gifts is like solving your own tiny mystery!

People Enjoy Mystery

People enjoy mystery. Mystery keeps you curious and entertained. Mystery teases you to solve the unknown, taunting you with promises of secrets yet unrevealed.

Mystery has kept people entertained since time began, always challenging people to answer basic fundamental life questions, such as:

What shape is the Earth?

What causes rain to fall from the sky?

Where does the sun go during the night?

Where does the moon go during the day?

Does the sun orbit around the moon?

At one time these were profound questions that stimulated debate and controversy. People devoted lifelines to answering these questions. Today the answers are taken for granted. As with all things, the controversy faded as the mystery faded.

All Knowledge Already Exists

All knowledge already exists. There is only one pool of knowledge, sitting there, waiting to be "discovered." Electricity existed before humankind discovered it. Fire existed before it was discovered. The transmission of sound waves through radio, telephone, and television existed before it was manifested into this dimension. The mystery for humankind was to find the correct clues to bring information forward into the collective conscious mind.

The **challenge** of unraveling the mysteries teaches people. Electricity itself is not mysterious, nor is fire, nor is the transmission of sound waves. A specific set of questions had to be asked to open the doors to that knowledge.

The explorers of human thought opened those doors through the process of trial and error. They found the correct combination of questions that allowed them to access a deeper level of knowledge. They did not find "new" knowledge. They tapped into existing knowledge, adding the perspective of known knowledge.

The Correct Combination Of Questions

Every person is in the middle of his/her own private mystery. Each individual must find the correct combination of questions to unravel his/her own personal puzzle. A set of questions must be developed to lead into untapped knowledge. In turn, expanding upon those questions takes one into even deeper levels of knowledge. This continues to be a lifelong process of questions and answers, trial and error. Think of this in terms of opening a combination lock. No matter how many numbers you turn to, the lock does not open until all the correct numbers are known in the correct order.

The Mysteries Are For You

The mysteries are there for your entertainment, enjoyment, and fulfillment. You already have all the clues you need. You simply work with those clues until they give order and meaning to your particular mystery.

In the same way, a crossword puzzle contains all of its own answers. The puzzle is filled with clues, including the number of letters per word. Each correct word is an additional clue for the next word. An "et" here or a "ra" there may not tell you anything for the moment. But each is a clue that leads to another question. The correct combination of questions leads to the correct answer. Eventually, the "et's" and "ra's" make sense. And, finally, the puzzle is finished.

You Are A Mystery In Miniature

As a microcosm of the macrocosm, you are a mystery in miniature. You need the correct combination of questions to take you into your very own answers. Solving the pieces to your own puzzle automatically allows the grand mystery to unfold. The same rules apply to both the microcosm and the macrocosm—in each case, the answers come in bits and pieces.

Eventually, you will have the big picture. But for now, take the pieces that you find. No matter how small, file them away for later use. Remember, the entertainment is in the process of solving the mystery. The answer is the prize for working the process correctly.

Life itself is open, simple, and clean. People are the ones who surround it with mystery and intrigue. The answers are already there. Sometimes it is so simple that it only appears complex and elusive.

Art Imitates Life

Serial television shows are wonderful examples of how easy it is to complicate life's simple situations. The process of how people set their own life circumstances in motion are blatantly detailed in serial shows. They are excellent examples of how simple situations quickly become complicated and messy.

Serial shows often reflect real life in their own exaggerated way. Use them as a study tool. Ask yourself if they reflect any part of your life. If you have an adverse reaction to these types of shows, search for deeper meaning, because it may be a clue that you are avoiding! Remember, only when your reaction to a situation is neutral are you really finished with it.

Horizontal/Vertical Experiences

The mysteries will unravel even faster when you choose vertical experiences over horizontal ones.

Definition: Vertical experiences pull you *up* into *new* growth.

Definition: Horizontal experiences pull you *out* into *similar* growth.

For example, say you are vice president of a company. Another company offers you a job with the same title and level of responsibility. This move is a horizontal one. Going from company to company as vice president brings the same types of experiences. Although each vice presidency will vary somewhat, the general job description remains the same.

However, a move from vice president to president to chief executive officer is vertical growth. Each position moves you upward in your learning experiences. Each step up broadens your knowledge. Each time you learn the previous position well before you are offered the next vertical position.

Everyone has many horizontal experiences. You may belong to six local service organizations. If they bring you the same types of experiences, they are horizontal experiences. However, belonging to a local, county, and state service organization may provide vertical experiences.

Consider the following analogy. Visualize a washcloth and label it "experience." Wring it until it is as dry as possible. Now think of each personal experience as that washcloth. Wring it dry for every drop of knowledge that it holds. Treating every experience in this way successfully establishes vertical growth.

Once you make a conscious decision to grow vertically, you may be surprised at the acceleration of your growth rate. You extract so much knowledge from each experience that you have fewer of the same types of experiences. This means you now have more correct combinations of questions that to move you faster into continually deeper levels of inner knowledge.

Understand your microcosm first. Know that it is the secret to understanding the macrocosm. As your personal mystery unravels, rules to the deeper mysteries automatically reveal themselves.

YOUR PERSONAL PUZZLE

*"Decide in conscious awareness the types of moments
that you want in your life."*

There are basic rules to follow when solving your own personal puzzle. The first one is easy to overlook because it sounds so simple—it is called observation.

All you have to do is learn to observe. You express who you are just by being. Your body language, tone of voice, colors you choose to wear, and home all reflect what is happening inside of yourself. Even the people that you choose to have in your life are reflections of yourself. These reflections teach you about yourself when you let them. But when you hurry through life you may overlook these key clues.

Organize Your Life Into Moments

Put the process in motion by slowing down long enough to allow each moment equal importance. This organizes your life into moments that you can observe and evaluate. A moment is a small fraction of time that you can deal with **right now**. Past years, months, weeks, and days all began in a moment. Organizing your moments automatically organizes your life.

For example, group happy moments together. Group peaceful moments together. Group satisfied moments together. Observe them, looking for the common action that led to these positive moments. Once you know, you can repeat these same types of moments in conscious awareness, allowing you to consciously bring more happy, peaceful, satisfied, etc., moments into your life.

In the same way, group your negative moments together. A significant other puts you down, then a friend rejects you. The pharmacist at the local drugstore verbally abuses you. Group these moments together. You had a common action that led to these similar results. Recall the previous moments to find the common action.

You may not be able to find the common action from only three incidents. That is okay. Continue to group similar moments together. Eventually, the common action will become obvious. This may take a long time, or it may happen quite rapidly.

Once you have a group of similar moments, you are on your way. Continue to observe them. Evaluate them for the similar actions that lead to similar results. With this knowledge, you can create less or more of any type of moment that you desire. Always look for the common actions that create similar events. Changing the common action changes the outcomes of the events in your life in conscious awareness.

View Your Life With Objectivity

The interesting part of observing is learning to do it objectively, without judgment or criticism of Self. This increases the intrigue and challenge. As the saying goes, "it is easier to solve someone else's problems than your own." That is because it is easier to step back and view another's life with objectivity.

Learning to be an objective observer of your own life means withdrawing the emotional involvement from your moments to make accurate evaluations. You need a clear picture of your life to make honest assessments of where you are and where you want to go. Become the subject of your own study.

Work From Your Center

You need a home base from which to work; a place that is safe and comfortable; a place that you can take with you wherever you go. That place is your center, which you began in **Section I** in the chapter, *Into the Silence.*

With your breath, will yourself into it any time that you feel scattered and/or uncomfortable. Feel the deep inner connection to your Oversoul and God-Mind. Feel the strength that is yours to claim. Know that as long as you remain in your center, you are safe. From your center, you can look at anything that you choose to express knowing that it is your action, but it is not you. You are separate from your actions because you are the actor/actress on the stage.

You can make any decision that you want while in your center. But, whatever you choose to express, either positive or negative, do it in conscious awareness. If you want to keep negative moments in your life, do not hide this decision from yourself. Be honest. Be negative, but do it in awareness. Then observe the consequences of those moments. Continue to evaluate what you want in your life and why.

You may not be ready to let go of the negative moments. This is perfectly acceptable. However, do acknowledge their existence as well as your role in maintaining them. If you choose to keep them, then grow by allowing them to teach you. When the time comes, you will let them go.

For example, you may need attention, so you choose to hold onto medical conditions. You may be filled with anger, so you may choose to hold onto explosive relationships. You may feel powerless, so you choose to hang onto control and manipulation to give yourself a feeling of power. All of these experiences began with one negative moment and now exist as a combination of many negative moments. It is your choice whether to hold onto these negative moments, or release them.

To start the process, use your breath to will yourself into your center. Watch your actions and words as though it were the first time that you ever met yourself. Start playing the role of an objective observer with these questions:

What is your opinion of this person?

Is this person someone who you would like to know?

Would you enjoy his/her company?

What is the tone of his/her voice?

What kind of emotions does he/she express, and when?

How does he/she treat his/her body?

How does he/she treat his/her material world?

How does he/she interact with other people?

Become Your Own Video Camera

Become your own video camera that is in the process of recording yourself only for the purpose of evaluation. Do not judge or criticize. Only observe and gather data to get an accurate, unbiased look at your moments. Observe yourself being happy, calm, peaceful, hardworking, punctual, easy-going; sad, angry, irritated, lazy, late, tense. The list can go on and on. These are examples of actions that are separate from you. As you observe, ask yourself these questions:

What do I think of these actions?

Do I want more or less of these types of actions in my life?

Do I like myself when I act like this?

How do other people respond when I act like this?

How important are these types of actions to me?

Am I willing to let any of them go?

Use this information to make accurate decisions about which types of moments you want to keep and which ones you no longer need. As you gather the data, pass them up the channel to your Oversoul. This moves your energy vertically, preparing you for vertical growth. Releasing what you already know further opens the doors to inner knowledge.

When you first start observing yourself, it may be difficult to watch yourself express emotions and actions that you would rather not see. Your first reaction may be to judge and criticize. You most likely have established vibratory imprints of Self-criticism and Self-judgment which took time to build, so expect to take some time to dismantle them.

Release Judgment Of Self

Self-criticism and Self-judgment are a natural part of the process. You may even find yourself criticizing and judging yourself because you are criticizing and judging yourself! If you do, merely acknowledge your actions in an objective way. For instance, you could say:

"Here I go, criticizing and judging myself again. I release my criticisms and judgments up to my Oversoul. In return, I ask for understanding of my actions. I also ask for alternative avenues of action to replace the ones that I am in the process of releasing."

You are **in the process** of learning how to be non-critical and non-judgmental of Self. Although that is your goal, you are not there yet. You are just now learning the necessary steps to get there, so it does not make sense to chastise yourself. Simply acknowledge that you are being critical and judgmental. Release those feelings up to your Oversoul. Move into the observing stage as best as you can.

Any new action feels awkward at first. With practice, observing yourself objectively becomes easier. The old vibratory imprint weakens while the new imprint gains strength.

Remember to observe from your center. Also remember that your emotions and actions are separate from you. They are not you; they cannot consume you. Remain in your center instead of fully participating in a no-longer-desired behavior pattern. As you separate yourself from these emotions and actions, they become easier to watch. As a result your evaluations become more accurate.

All information that you gather about yourself is equally important. Negative information tells you about your weak areas. Positive information denotes your strengths. Use the positive to buttress your weak areas. Take a moment to thank your Oversoul for the people and experiences that bring these weak areas to your attention. Without them, you would not be aware of your weaknesses.

Make Changes Now

Because you are in a constant state of growth, everything that goes into you eventually moves out of you. Experiences come into your life from your Oversoul, leaving a vibratory imprint. Sooner or later, the vibratory imprint returns to your Oversoul, so take the initiative to move it out in conscious awareness.

Objective observing gives you the opportunity to release the negatives in conscious awareness. Your alternative may be to have it forced out of you at some later point in time. This is your chance to make changes now in the least uncomfortable way possible.

The observing process shows you any preconceived ideas of who you are, what you express, and how you choose to express it. Objective observing provides the opportunity to find out if who you **really** are matches the picture of who you **think** you are.

You may be surprised at the differences in the illusions that you have versus the reality of what is. You may find that there are parts of yourself that are not as "bad" as you thought. You may also find that there are parts that are not as "wonderful" as you

100

thought. Do your best to remain as objective as possible, no matter what you discover. Change your attitude—

from
"Oh no, here I go again!"
to
"Oh boy, here I grow again!"

Always acknowledge that you are where you are supposed to be with the tools and experiences that you have. Objective observing means stating the facts—what does or does not exist:

I am irritated.

She irritates me.

The situation irritates me.

The above examples only acknowledge fact. There is no criticism or judgment involved. Once you state the facts, then you can evaluate, and move from there. Go slowly, without undue pressure on yourself. Continue moving forward as best as you can.

Let Others Teach You

As you observe yourself moment by moment, you become aware of why you act and react the way that you do. This in turn clarifies others' actions and reactions toward you. Remember, you express who you are simply by being.

Others react to that expression, whether they are aware of it or not. They react to your body language, tone of voice, colors you choose to wear, and the contents of your aura. They process this information extremely quickly on an unconscious level of awareness, usually oblivious to its effect upon them.

Act In Conscious Awareness

Slowing down the process allows you to act in conscious awareness. You become aware of everything that you choose to project, moment by moment. This means you make conscious decisions about the colors you wear, words you speak, tone of voice, gestures, and what you keep in your aura.

Now you can understand why people react to you as they do. If their reactions disturb you, ask these questions:

What can I change so that others react to me differently?

Which one of my qualities are they showing me?

What are they teaching me about myself?

The people that you choose to have around you reflect who you are. If you do not like their actions, then it is your puzzle to find out what **you** can change within to change that reflection.

An Objective Observer

An objective observer sees, hears, touches, tastes, and smells with great acuity. The senses heighten as you process all available information. Your analysis of any given moment becomes exceptionally accurate.

Over time, Self-observations become less judgmental and critical, making it easier to release undesired behavior with less attachment to your actions. You develop a softer, gentler attitude toward yourself as you release the harsh judge. It is replaced with understanding and compassion for Self. In turn, others reflect that softer, gentler attitude back to you.

As an objective observer, you now have a method to sort and organize your life. Do it moment by moment, slowly and methodically. Group similar moments with similar moments. Through observation, identify the similar actions that led to similar results. Decide in conscious awareness the types of moments you want in your life. And make conscious decisions of how you want to put them there.

What Did You Say?

"Never overlook the simplicity of the beginning point."

Inner listening is very simple. The secret is to start by listening to yourself. Listen objectively, without judgment or criticism. Listen only for the purpose of gathering data and making evaluations. Breathe yourself into your center, and observe yourself as the objective listener. For instance, listen to the tone of your voice. Ask yourself, is it: pleasant? gentle? kind? calm? harsh? overbearing? sharp? too quiet? too loud?

What does your tone express? contentment? peacefulness? happiness? understanding? anger? resentment? sadness? insecurity? guilt?

Choose Empowering Words

Pay attention to the words that you choose. If you listen to them, they will teach you about your state of inner being. Listen for phrases that weaken body, mind, or spirit. Choose to release the need for words that do not affirm the positive in your life. Listen to the words that you choose. Do they affirm the positive or negative in your life? For example:

I am trying to learn how to improve myself.
Trying is not the same as doing.

I am afraid that I am going to be late.
This is a statement of inner being.

I can't afford not to go to class.
Are you holding back abundance with this phrase?

I am sick and tired of hearing you complain.
What does this phrase contribute to your health?

I can't stand it.
Back, feet, or legs giving you any problem?

I hate being late.
Do you hate?

I don't deserve this wonderful surprise.
What *do* you deserve?

The words that you have chosen for many years, perhaps many lifelines, set the patterns into motion that you live today. The words that you chose yesterday, a few minutes ago, set up the experiences of today, of this moment. You constantly live your past.

Match Words With Feelings

Do your words match what you feel inside?

Do your words say that you are happy when you truly are not?

Do you say that one thing frustrates you when it is really something else?

Do you complain about your current circumstances when there is a part of you that enjoys it?

Observe Body Language

Observe your body language as you speak:

What gestures do you make?

When do you make them?

Do your gestures match your words and/or inner feelings?

Your body language tells you about yourself. On some level of awareness, it also tells others about you. When words match tone of voice, feelings, and body language, they convey a much stronger and clearer message.

Talking Without Listening

You can easily talk without really listening to yourself. Words sometimes just tumble out while your mind wanders elsewhere. People react to the lack of attention that you pay to your own words. Why should they listen if you do not care enough to listen to yourself?

Are you the only one participating in the conversation? Are you: rambling? repeating the same story? bored with your own conversation? getting too personal? offering unwanted advice? talking about something that the other person cares nothing about?

Remember, gather the data for evaluation purposes only. If you start judging or criticizing yourself, simply acknowledge this. Then pass those feelings on up to your Oversoul.

Objectively Listen

Because the outer always reflects the inner, objectively listen to others when they speak. Their tone of voice, words that they choose, and body language all reflect some part of you—past, present, or future.

Objectively listen and let the other person teach you. Too often, people actively engage in talking to themselves instead of conversing with each other. While one speaks, the other is busy thinking about what he/she will say next. When you think about the conversation later, it is much easier to recall what you said, how you said it, and how clever you were. It is much more difficult to recall what the other person said.

Do not listen to judge or criticize, but to let others reflect you back to yourself. If they ramble consistently, you better check yourself for the same quality. If they are boring, then ask yourself to notice when you are boring. If they are judgmental or critical, look to see where you might be judgmental or critical.

Objectively listen to others. Use the same list of questions that you apply to yourself. Then use that knowledge to objectively listen to yourself.

Whenever anyone speaks to you, there is a reason. They take time to show you something about yourself. Therefore, evaluate everything that is spoken to you for validity. Even words spoken in anger might force you to face an area of yourself that you are avoiding. When someone is angry with you, it catches your attention. Those same words spoken in kindness might not be heard.

Always evaluate any accusations, judgments, criticisms, observations, or off-handed comments. Perhaps they are valid remarks. Or perhaps this is a chance for you to stand up for yourself. Tell your Oversoul that you will listen as long as these experiences are explained to your satisfaction.

Selective Listening

Sometimes on an unconscious level of awareness you pick and choose only what you **want** to hear. This is called "selective listening." What you decide to listen to and retain usually perpetuates your Self-illusions. These illusions can be either positive or negative. In your mind is a picture of who you think you are. If what you hear does not match that picture, you may not retain any of that conversation.

For instance, someone may pay you a compliment that you think is not deserved. You may not really hear or remember it because you do not think that it is valid. Or, suppose six people compliment a project that you feel good about. Then one person makes a casual off-handed remark that indicates the project is inferior.

You may choose to remember that one remark if you retain an illusion of low Self-worth. You can choose to use that comment to nurture your illusions. Or, you can choose to use it as a growth tool. The person who spoke those words provided a test for you. Pull yourself into your center. Use that opportunity as a chance to acknowledge your Self-worth.

Listen Through Your Oversoul

Listen to others through your Oversoul. As they speak, ask your Oversoul to explain their words to you. As you push your energy up through the channel, ask your Oversoul:

What is the feeling behind the words?

What is this person *really* saying to me?

What does this person *really* want to know from me?

Direct the energy of your words up to your Oversoul. Then, ask your Oversoul to direct both your spoken and unspoken words.

Levels Of Listening

Objective listening automatically takes you deeper inside, moving you into new levels of inner awareness. As a natural part of the process, you hear with greater clarity. Your mind becomes more focused and directed.

The following are different ways one listens:

Words

Feelings

Energy

Color

Vibration

Words

People most often associate listening with words. Words on the outer level are important. They direct your attention, giving you a reference point for communication. However, as you move into the deeper levels of listening, you find that there are no words. Words as you commonly think of them are not always necessary.

Feelings

Behind the words are feelings. Feelings come first. Words are then attached to explain those feelings. Observe people who grope for the "right" words to explain their experiences. They often first make a series of hand gestures that depict feelings. They may even spit and stutter a little as they work to find those "right" words.

When this occurs, take the opportunity to listen through your Oversoul. Ask your Oversoul to explain the feelings before they become spoken words. This helps you connect with the level of feeling.

As you practice, others may label you "psychic." But all you are doing is objectively listening to the feelings that are already present. You are not doing anything unusual or strange. You are only aware of what exists **right now**. Your Oversoul explains your evaluations.

As an added thought, recognize that you are in the process of moving beyond psychic, or personal energy. When you allow others to label you psychic, they confine you to that level. Using universal energy takes you into the level of "knowing by knowing." Keep true to your goal without stopping in the process.

Energy

Feelings are comprised of energy. They have form and consistency. Listen to the energy that you use behind the words that you speak. Feel it, passing those feelings up to your Oversoul. Using the following sample questions, ask your Oversoul to direct your learning:

Is the energy clear? muddy?

Does the energy have solidity? strength? holes? webs?

What kind of weight does the energy have horizontal weight? vertical weight?

The feel of the energy behind the words tells many things. When you "puff" up your stories, this is exactly what happens to your energy. It comes out of your mouth in puffs and floats away.

When you do not know what you are talking about the energy is full of holes. Muddy energy may contain a lie. Boring energy feels horizontal. On the other hand, truth feels strong, solid, and clear.

Color

The psychic energy with which people speak has color. The feeling behind the words and combination of words create wave lengths of color.

You may not be able to see the colors with your physical eyes, but you can feel them. Begin to associate words, feelings, and energy with color. Feel when they match, keeping in mind that all color has both positive and negative qualities.

Read through the following examples. Observe the feelings while visualizing the hue of the colors used in each example.

Negative: His yellow streak is showing.
Positive: He has a golden moment.

Negative: She is so mad she sees red.
Positive: She has a red-letter day.

Negative: He is green with jealousy.
Positive: He has a green thumb.

Recognize that the negative statements have a heavy feeling while the positive statements have a light feeling. Negative hues tend to be dark and cloudy. Positive ones tend to be lighter and clearer.

Objectively listen, feeling the color of your own words. Ask your Oversoul to direct the learning process with the following questions:

What color are my words? a clear color? a muddy color? Is it important that I know?

The energy and colors of a conversation change as subjects change. Communication with others is most effective when you both speak in the same color. When you speak in orange and the other person speaks in blue, you have difficulty communicating. Communicating on the "same wave length" is important.

As you converse, visualize what you think the colors might be. Keep passing your observations up to your Oversoul while asking these questions:

Does the color of my words match the color of his/her words?

Do I want the colors to match?
(Changing the color of your words changes the conversation.)

Am I getting my point across?
(Ask your Oversoul to match the colors for you.)

Everyone reacts to the color of words on some level of awareness. If someone chooses to take an ego trip at your expense, you may react to the sharpness of his/her bright orange words. To end the conversation, speak to him/her in a different color. If it is your boss, you may choose to speak back in orange, allowing the ego-boosting conversation to continue!

Right now, merely be aware that color is a function of listening. When you **need** to understand, you will.

Vibration

The next level of listening is vibration. The vibratory imprints of past experiences surround every person. These vibratory imprints contain your past, present, and the future that you are in the process of creating. As your objective listening skills develop, tune into your own vibratory imprints. Listen to them. They will relate whatever events your Oversoul wishes you to know.

Listen to your vibratory imprints during meditation. Breathe yourself into your center. Ask your Oversoul to tell you who and what you are. Tell your Oversoul to prepare you for the answers.

As you move into ever-deeper levels of inner listening, let your Oversoul teach you. It will always show you whatever you **need** to know. This is different from what you might **want** to know. Trust the wisdom of your Oversoul.

Inner Listening

The process of inner listening begins in the present. Tone of voice, words that you choose, and body language are all known knowledge. Study what you have in front of you **right now.** Understanding known knowledge leads into your own previously untapped knowledge.

Never overlook the simplicity of the beginning point. Appreciate what you have instead of criticizing and/or judging yourself for what you do not have. When you appreciate your present moment, it teaches you. Your present moment provides the answers and the questions that move you deeper inside of yourself, closer to who you really are.

Moving Forward

"A decision to change begins with a thought. The success of your change depends on the strength of that thought."

As you organize and observe your moments, you have some decisions to make:

Which actions do I want to keep?
Which actions am I ready to discard?
How do I make these decisions?

And finally, the most important question of all:

How do I feel about change?

Change is one of those processes that is often easier to talk about than to implement.

Change means—
moving out of the status quo.
moving out of your comfort zone and into unfamiliar territory.
actively pursuing new avenues of action.
putting yourself and your capabilities on the line.
taking risks.

All of the above means that at some point you may feel awkward, insecure, foolish, and/or inadequate. Even change that you recognize as positive can be a threat. You can no longer rely on old habit responses to get you through new challenges. Looking for the adventure in a new experience may be difficult when you feel the discomfort that an unfamiliar one brings.

Are you willing to—
be flexible?
release the old?
move through your fears?

accept and implement the new?
assume responsibility for deeper knowledge?

Each person can only hold a given number of experiences. You can choose to hold onto the old, familiar ones. Or, you can choose to release them. Releasing them allows new experiences rich with knowledge to enter your life.

Your search for Self is a process of moving through the known into the unknown. Moving into the unknown means accessing different knowledge. This changes you, your reactions, and your outer world's reactions. This also brings greater responsibility.

Responsibility

What will do with your "new" knowledge? Will you use it to help others or manipulate them? To understand or criticize? To progress on your journey or impress others? Responsibility comes with knowledge. A deeper awareness of the mysteries of life makes you more accountable for your actions.

Compare this to the laws of society. A child who takes a candy bar without paying may not realize that society calls this stealing. When caught, the act may only warrant a firm explanation. But a child who takes a candy bar with the knowledge that it is stealing will have greater consequences.

As further explanation, pretend that you tap into knowledge that allows you to heal everyone you touch. Does this give you permission to run through all the hospitals healing everyone you see?

This would probably give you a great feeling of Self-importance. People everywhere would beg for your attention. Is this your goal? Where would this put you on your path? Because you **can** do something, does that give you permission to do it indiscriminately?

All knowledge brings responsibility. With illness comes lessons. If you take away illness indiscriminately, you may take away the only chance some people have to learn. However, there may be others your Oversoul will direct you to heal. They have learned their lessons. They just need a little help to move into their next level of awareness. Work with your Oversoul. Ask your Oversoul to give you the wisdom to correctly use whatever knowledge is revealed to you.

Attitude Is Important

Your attitude toward change is important. Your objective observations and listening skills teach you about yourself with honesty. Be honest with yourself about what you really **want** to change.

Identify something that you would like to change. Start the process by asking the following questions:

Do I really **want** to change it?
> **or**
Do I just think that I **should** change it?

There is a difference. For example, do you really **want** to give up smoking? Or do you just think that you **should**? If you truly do not want to give it up, why spend time fighting against yourself? Without criticism or judgment of Self, simply acknowledge that for now you like to smoke. When the time is right, you will give it up. For now, choose something else. Focus your energy on something that you really want to change.

An Exchange With Change

Next, recognize that there is always an exchange with change.

Consider these examples:
    You must give up money to purchase a sofa.
    You must give up the old sofa to make room for the new one.
    You must give up sickness along with its perks, for health.
    You must give up anger, bitterness, and resentment for peace of mind.

No matter what you decide to change, you will always give up something in exchange. This may be a major factor in your decision to make changes. Ask the following questions:

What will I lose by changing?
What will I gain by changing?

Decide if what you will gain outweighs what you will lose. If any part of you does not want to let go, acknowledge it. Then pass those feelings up to your Oversoul. Move forward with your change.

Three Steps To Change

There are three basic steps to change:

Trying

The first step is **trying**. The old vibratory imprint is still strong, and seems to have a mind of its own. The old vibratory imprint pulls you the moment you look the other direction.

You **try** to loosen its strength. You **try** to establish a new imprint, but it is still young and weak. Affirmations are extremely important at this time. They establish new feelings in your aura. Use them often to continually strengthen the new imprint.

Prepare yourself to be pulled back into the old vibratory imprint. Do not criticize yourself when this happens. Observe when it happens, realizing that this is a natural part of the process of change. Evaluate how you can act differently the next time. Release all of your feelings up to your Oversoul.

Becoming

The next step in the process is **becoming**. The old vibratory imprint is weakening. You release more of it up to your Oversoul. Affirmations are still important, but not as mandatory. The new vibratory imprint is strengthening.

This is a transition period. You may find yourself in a "push-me, pull-me" situation, not totally comfortable with the new, yet no longer comfortable with the old. You may even feel like giving up the change. Yet, deep down you know that you cannot go back.

During this stage, the old vibratory imprint pulls you back less often. You still fall into it from time to time, but it is losing its strength.

Being

The last and final step is *being*. The old vibratory imprint is totally broken up and released to your Oversoul. The new vibratory imprint is strong and established, functioning in accordance with the way that you built it. Affirmations are no longer necessary. You no longer have to *try*. You just *are*. The new vibratory imprint is expressed in the way you speak, your mannerisms, and your overall attitudes.

Creative Thinking

Sometimes after identifying a change that you really want to make, you may have difficulty deciding how to make it. Your mind may seem locked into one pattern of behavior that runs you around in circles *trying* to find a new solution to an old situation.

You may need some practice in the area of creative thinking. Do this by stimulating new areas of your brain to induce new methods of thinking. Start small and be successful. Begin the process simply by doing ordinary tasks in extraordinary ways. This breaks up old habit responses that result from old vibratory imprints, and stimulates new areas of your brain. You can:

Wear your watch on the "other" arm.

Sleep on the "other" side of the bed.

Eat with your "other" hand.

Drink your morning coffee from a different cup.

Drive to work using a different route.

Park in a different parking space.

Anything that breaks up regular routines forces you to think differently. New brain cells are stimulated into action. These simple activities allow new avenues of action to filter into your conscious mind.

Creative thinking sets the stage for change. These small changes allow you to associate new feelings with success. Thus you gain confidence to attempt larger, more significant changes.

The thought of a major change can sometimes be overwhelming. You may procrastinate so long that you never begin. Fear of failure (or of success!) leads you to do nothing.

So, start in the beginning to establish a new vibratory imprint that says:

Change is possible.

Change is acceptable.

Change can be fun and exciting.

Start small, and feel good about your progress. Take one step at a time. If one step is too threatening, then take a half-step, or a quarter-step. Change in a way that is comfortable for you.

Change May Threatens Others

Your change may threaten others. As you change, others must change their reactions to you. Any change you make automatically forces them out of their comfort zones and into unfamiliar territory.

Suddenly, others may find themselves in new growth patterns that they may not be consciously prepared to accept. Because this takes them out of their status quo, they may try to sabotage your change. This might be a conscious or unconscious reaction.

For instance, you finally decide to lose that extra weight. You start a strict diet, thinking your family and friends will be thrilled. As you lose the weight, your spouse begins to feel insecure. He/she wonders if he/she will remain the most important person in your life. He/she starts tempting you with all your favorite foods.

Your best friend becomes jealous because he/she thinks that you look better than he/she does. Your friendship becomes strained and uncomfortable. Both your spouse and friend rebel against your positive change. They may not consciously be aware that your change causes their insecurities to surface.

For this reason, it is always important to share your plans with others on the inner levels. Explain to them through their Oversouls what changes you are in the process of making and why. Explain fears and frustrations, while acknowledging their right to be afraid. Know that on some level they realize that your change means their change.

Remember, you will always have people around you who best reflect you to yourself. Either they must change to continue that reflection, or drop out of your life. Respect their struggles.

All You Have Is A Thought

A decision to change begins with a thought. The success of your change depends upon the strength of that thought. Thoughts create the energy that moves you into and through a change.

Your original thought is a seed of energy. Every time you think about making the change, you produce similar thoughts. These similar thoughts are drawn to that energy seed. This process gathers "thought" energy.

When you collect enough "thought" energy, change begins. However, it is possible to lose that energy if you:

Speak too soon.
or
Act too soon.

Every time you speak, you disperse energy. Speaking too soon about a planned change weakens the seed. It must wait for more thoughts to regain its strength. Talking about a plan of action in its early stage of energy gathering weakens the plan. Continuing to talk about it may mean that enough energy never accumulates to follow through with an action. You are probably familiar with the saying, "He's all talk and no action." This is why.

For this reason, speak very little about your plans. Advise others via the involved Oversouls, but keep as much "thought" energy as possible to yourself. Use it to accomplish your goals.

Accumulated energy can also be dispersed by acting too soon. Gather enough "thought" energy to propel you on through to your goals. Affirmations add energy to the seed thought. Reading books that enforce your goals also helps. Even the company that you keep strengthens the process. Be among people who pull you up into your potential.

Correct Timing

Determine the correct timing for action. Rely on what you know about feeling before you speak or act. When you speak or act too soon, remember the feeling. When you speak or act and everything flows smoothly, remember that feeling. These experiences build a data base for future reference.

Release the data base up to your Oversoul. Before you speak or act, ask your Oversoul if this is the correct timing. What feelings come back from your Oversoul? Your inner communications tell you when the timing is correct.

How Do I Feel About Change?

How you feel about change affects all the answers to all the questions that you will ask along your journey. Your capacity to change determines how deep within you will go.

Change means—

Growth.

Expansion.

Movement.

New and exciting experiences.

Embrace change. Enjoy the variety of experiences that it brings. Let it teach you about your depths yet unrevealed.

YOU HAVE A CHOICE

"Consciously build new habit responses that contain
more desirable patterns of behavior."

You choose your own words and actions. Other people or situations can only evoke behavior that already exists within you. No one can make you respond in any particular way unless you choose to do so.

Occasionally people get so locked into patterns of behavior they forget that they have choices. You do not have to respond to the same situations in the same ways unless you make that choice. For instance:

Are you grumpy when you wake up in the morning?

Does mowing the lawn irritate you?

Do you resent cleaning the house?

Are you angry at the morning traffic?

Are you impatient with your children?

All of the above are examples of "habit responses." You automatically feel a certain way. You automatically react to those feelings. You do not stop and question if you want those reactions in your life. You make your choices without thinking.

Definition: A habit response is an established pattern of behavior that allows you to react to any given situation without thinking—whether physical or mental; positive, negative, or neutral.

Physical Habit Responses

Walking is an example of a physical habit response. Learning to walk is a difficult task for a child. Maintaining balance, shifting weight at just the right time, and avoiding collisions with objects takes all of a child's concentration.

117

Eventually, walking becomes a habit response. This habit response allows children to walk at will, freeing them to talk, carry things, and eat while walking. An adult no longer has to think about how to walk. An adult simply walks.

Mental Habit Responses

Mental habit responses develop in the same way. They also allow you to react without thinking. When you see your neighbor working in her yard you automatically smile and say hello. Your son running through the house automatically makes you snap at him to slow down. You really do not put much thought into either activity. Having done it before, you most likely will do it again.

Habit Responses Are Comfortable

Habit responses are comfortable. They just sit there, waiting for you to use them. Habit responses are ready responses. They are tried-and-true courses of action. You know how you will react. You can "predict" how others will react.

Your neighbor smiles back and says hello. Your son momentarily slows down. Without interrupting your lifestyle, you have ready responses to familiar situations. For many situations, this is fine.

Old Habit Responses

In most instances habit responses start off innocently. You use a course of action once and it works. The next time a similar situation arises you use it again. The next thing you know, you have a habit response. These habit responses serve a purpose for a time. They add efficiency to your life.

However, as you change you may forget to reprogram your habit responses. You may continue to rely on habit responses that are no longer appropriate. Accustomed to using them without thinking, you may fail to realize what you do and why.

Evaluate some of your own habit responses to determine if they are still useful. Think about situations that always evoke similar responses. Do you have a habit of speaking harshly? Do you have an underlying pattern of bitterness and resentment? If so, why? Where did it come from?

Do you have a habit of wringing your hands? Is this a sign of tension in other areas of your life? What can you do to relieve that tension?

Do you have a habit of being late? Is it because you are accustomed to getting attention in a negative way? Are you ready to release negative attention?

Do you have a habit of not liking your physical body? What part do you not like? When did you stop liking it and why? Is it time to let those feelings go?

You may be surprised at how often you react without knowing why. Words pop out of your mouth. Actions just occur. Pay attention to what you do and why. Acknowledge and label your actions to increase your ability to choose in conscious awareness.

Now ask yourself:

Could I react to these situations differently?

Do I want to?

Would my life be more pleasant?

Would I feel better about myself?

Take the time to stop and think before you react to make room for options and choices. Even stopping and thinking after-the-fact is progress. At least you are aware of what you did. You can evaluate the situation and decide how you would like to react the next time. Eventually, you will stop and think before you react.

Habit responses exist whether you choose to use them or not. For this reason, it is important to identify and evaluate them. Release the ones that you no longer need up to your Oversoul.

Habit Responses Are Interconnected

Habit responses are often interconnected. Fear is a good example.
You may have fear of:

heights.

knives.

airplanes.

water.

not finishing in time.

looking foolish.

not being good enough.

your children hurting themselves.

At first glance, all of these situations might appear to be entirely different. But reading through the list, you easily see that they all relate to the habit response of fear. Fear feeds upon fear; fear builds upon fear. These experiences are definitely interconnected.

Weakening fear any way possible weakens the vibratory imprint that holds the habit response in place. Releasing fear of knives weakens all fears, thus depleting the energy from an already strong habit response.

Moving through fear instead of using fear as a reaction stops adding strength to your habit response. Changing your reaction to one fear creates a positive chain reaction until

119

one day you will get on an airplane and suddenly realize that you are no longer afraid. Fear dissipates itself from lack of nourishment.

Build New Habit Responses

Consciously build new habit responses that contain desirable patterns of behavior. Use affirmations to help you. Affirmations create new feelings within, establishing a foundation for new patterns of behavior. Each time you affirm a positive habit response, you increase its strength. Eventually you automatically react in a positive way.

These new habit responses contain desirable reactions that match your current level of development. They redefine your life in a positive way. Consciously choose habit responses that affirm:

I speak gently.

I am healthy.

I experience abundance.

I have loving, comfortable relationships.

I appreciate all activities in my life.

I am peaceful and calm inside.

I am thankful for all that I have.

Release the habit responses that you no longer need. Choose to build new ones that recreate your life in a positive way. Remember, you have a choice.

MOVING THROUGH ILLUSION

"Knowledge changes illusion and reality. There will always be possibilities beyond what you perceive."

Illusion is important, allowing you to play-act through life. After all, you are only an actor/actress on a stage in this grand illusion called "life." Before birth, you choose the role that you want to play. Then you choose the country, race, and parents that create that role.

Your name, age, occupation, race, and religion are all part of your illusion. They describe a particular role at a particular moment in time and space.

As neutral energy, you exist beyond physical birth through physical death. Your physical body changes lifeline after lifeline. Yet **you** remain an evolutionizing constant. You encompass a time frame that equals infinity.

Expand Your Definition Of Self

The following questions may begin to move forward into your conscious mind as you expand your definition of Self:

What experiences brought me to this point in time?

How did my thoughts, feelings, and attitudes develop?

What influenced and shaped me?

What strengthened me?

What weakened me?

Why are specific people in my life?

What other dimensions am I experiencing?

These questions have a multitude of answers depending upon how deeply inside you take them. There are many layers of illusion, accumulated from this lifeline and others. These illusions have entertained and fascinated you for eons. They are a part of the process of God-Mind learning about God-Mind.

The deeper you go, the more layers you penetrate. Moving through layer upon layer of illusion brings you closer to reality. You are in the process of acquiring the necessary tools to move beyond illusion and into reality.

Exchange Illusion For Reality

Moving through illusion sounds easy on paper. However, remember there is always an exchange with change. If you give up illusion, what do you get in return? Reality.

Illusion leaves the process open; the possibilities are endless. Reality states fact. This can be frightening. Moving through illusion into a layer of reality means new knowledge. New knowledge means responsibility and change. Many people do not progress when they realize this.

Illusion allows you to make up the answers to your own questions. Illusion is only limited by your imagination. **Knowing** the answers moves you directly into reality. Reality is an entirely different matter.

To illustrate this point, think about this. You apply for a job that you really want. As long as you hear nothing, there is still a possibility that you will be hired. Even though the waiting is tedious, there is hope. However, with the answer comes reality. Either yes or no. There is no more illusion, only fact.

Take the shape of the Earth as another example. At one time it was accepted as fact that the earth was flat. People speculated and discussed at great length about what lay beyond the edge. Theologians speculated that hell lay just over the edge. Artists painted pictures of the dragons and demons that they thought lived beyond the edge of the Earth. The illusion of a flat Earth provided entertainment.

As support of the round Earth theory grew, exploration began. Moving through illusion, it was discovered that the Earth was indeed round. The reality of a round Earth opened new areas of discussion and thought. As known knowledge changed, the entertainment changed. Theologians had to find another place for hell to exist. Artists had to find other subjects to paint. It was time to move forward.

Illusion And Reality Function Side By Side

Illusion and reality often function side by side. This sometimes makes it difficult to distinguish between the two.

Definition: Illusion is the way you perceive things to be.

Reality is the way things really are. Reality may vary considerably from your perception of the way you think things are.

Most people, for example, intently project the positive part of themselves. They **try** to create the illusion that they only contain positive emotions, thoughts, words, and actions. They purposely suppress their negative side, **trying** to create an illusion for you—perhaps even for themselves. However, the reality is that people are dual-natured. They have positive and negative dimensions.

People work hard to create illusions. Families create illusions that tell the outside world that they are happy and stable. The reality can be extremely different.

The advertising media takes great care to create illusions around their products to encourage you to buy them. Illusion tells you to use a specific soap to make you happy, give you lots of energy, and bring fun and friends into your life. And this is only the beginning! Reality explains that using that specific soap only means that your physical body will be clean.

Illusion says that a soul in a fifty year-old body is wiser than one in a thirty year-old body. Realizing that people exist beyond the time frame of the body, reality may be completely different. The thirty year old may be much further along in the evolutionary process.

Illusion tells people to eradicate crime. Reality explains that criminals are important. They provide the impetus for many people to grow. Because of them, law enforcement officers have the opportunity to learn many skills. These include defense, observation, concentration, teamwork, bravery, and compassion. Reality explains that criminals are equal in importance to law enforcement agencies.

Illusion tells people to eliminate disease. Yet doctors, nurses, pharmacies, drug companies, advertisers, researchers, and medical schools are a small sample of what would no longer be necessary without sick people. Reality explains that sick people are important to the health care profession.

Illusion Is Safe

Illusion is a safe place to be. You know who you are, how you act, how other people will act, and what your responses will be. Whether or not you like your life is inconsequential. What you have **right now** is the known. When you change, you move into the unknown. You have to think of new reactions to new people, activities, and situations. For this reason, it often feels safer to stay in illusion without searching for reality.

Reality brings with it a new perspective on old situations. The reality of a round Earth opened up a new set of questions. Artists and theologians had to move out of the safe place that they created for themselves. They had to create new answers to old situations. In a way, the rug was pulled out from beneath them.

In the same way, it sometimes seems easier to remain in your comfort zone. Moving into reality means releasing the comfort of your illusions. You may find areas of Self that are not so great. Finding these areas means looking, feeling, and dealing with them. But, it also means finding the freedom that comes with removing Self-imposed limitations.

There is often a part of you that enjoys living in the comfort of illusion. That part is not at all interested in changing, and discourages you from moving through it to "reality." It tells you that illusion **is** reality, and works hard to keep you there. This part most likely contains many uncompleted and unresolved experiences. It tells you not to stir up painful memories that (you think) have been laid to rest long ago.

The reality, however, is that these memories live inside of you. Whether you are consciously aware of it or not, you react to your present through these memories. Sooner or later, they must be resolved.

As an example, you might feel you were unjustly punished as a child. At that time, it was not possible to express those feelings. Because they were never released, they still exist, creating tension within. To complete the experience, breathe yourself into your center. As an objective observer, allow the experience to surface, passing before your inner eye. Observe the emotions that you feel. Allow the part of you that contains these emotions to yell, scream, cry, or do whatever it needs for release, passing all feelings up to your Oversoul. Ask your Oversoul to pass these feelings along to all involved individuals via the appropriate Oversouls. On some level these people will receive your message.

Releasing these buried memories may cause some discomfort. Old scars must sometimes be opened to promote inner healing. To relive those memories takes a brave person. Realize that unresolved memories take up space within. Releasing them leaves room for peaceful feelings of inner harmony to grow.

Reality Explains

Illusion hides. Reality explains. A person who freely expresses anger toward you functions in an anger illusion. When you function in the same level of illusion, you express anger back. This contributes to the illusion that helps both of you understand anger.

Move through the illusion by being an objective observer and listener, instead of participating in it. Reality explains that it is the other person's own internal pain that creates the anger. Illusion tells that person to clean out the pain by giving it to others.

Reality explains that this is only a momentary buffer. Understanding the pain of this person allows you to have compassion for their inner struggles. You then no longer have to participate in this illusion because you understand beyond it. This moves you a layer closer to the reality of who you really are. Illusion entertains. However, there comes a point in all things when it is healthiest to move on.

Understand The Overall Plot

You did not create the play, but you are a participant within it. Illusion shows you only part of the script. Moving through illusion to reality is your real objective. This is vertical growth. Vertical growth allows you to see the play from above. From here, the overall plot is explained.

When you ask questions about reality, be sure that you pass them on up to your Oversoul and God-Mind. Remember, it is easy to get stuck in the space above your head that contains your own thoughts. Seeking answers from among your own thoughts limits those answers to the realm of known knowledge.

Reality explains that those answers must come from above, from your Oversoul and God-Mind. This expands your vision to new possibilities, moving you forward into "new" knowledge. Let the doors to the beyond open. Recognize that explanations exist that have not yet moved forward into your conscious mind, or perhaps into the mind of the entire collective conscious.

For instance, closing your mind to the possibility that criminals are a necessary part of the law enforcement play closes your mind to potential answers. Whenever you ask questions, be willing to hear the answers. Be willing to listen for answers that stretch you beyond current illusion and closer into reality. Your illusion of truth may be entirely different from the reality of truth.

Reality Expands And Grows

Reality expands and grows only as much as you let yourself grow. As you recognize and accept new ideas, reality explains that these concepts are infinitely deep.

As an example, say you start sculpting as a hobby. You learn the rules of sculpting that give it order. You accept the illusion that these rules cannot be broken or your project will fail. In effect, this illusion is your reality.

However, as you move deeper into the process you find that those rules **can** be broken, awakening the creativity within. Once you understand the basic beginning set of rules, you recognize that you can go beyond them with satisfactory, or even better results. This moves you closer to reality. As with all things, the more time you devote to sculpting, the more the process explains itself.

Initial illusion is important and an excellent beginning point. Moving through it with understanding moves you into the next levels of learning. Reality expands and grows in direct relation to your own growth.

Knowledge changes illusion and reality. There will always be possibilities beyond what you now perceive. This is what keeps you interested and entertained. Finding new solutions is fascinating as you focus on the process. Move through and beyond illusion, allowing reality to explain, slowly, one step at a time, and always with an open mind.

Experience Is Neutral

"Ask your Oversoul for help to move through the illusion of 'good' and 'bad,' into the reality that explains."

All experience is neutral. Your reactions to experience label it "good" or "bad." Positive reactions label experience "good." Negative reactions label experience "bad." Reality explains that all experience is actually neutral, just as you are neutral and God-Mind is neutral. Consider some of the following examples:

• *A small child is lost in the forest. He finds the forest intimidating and overwhelming. That child might describe the forest as dark, dreary, and lonely. Associating the forest with the feeling of being lost, he labels the forest "bad."*

On the other hand, as an adult he enjoys walking alone in the stillness of the forest. He associates the forest with feelings of peace and calm. Now, he labels the forest "good."

Question: Is the forest "good" or "bad?"

• *A carpenter lives in an economically depressed area. Work is difficult to find. He associates being a carpenter with lack of money. Eventually, he wonders if he chose the right profession. He labels the experience of being a carpenter "bad."*

Ten years later the same geographic area experiences growth. There is plenty of work. The carpenter is financially secure. He associates being a carpenter with success. Now, he labels the experience of being a carpenter "good."

Question: Is being a carpenter "good" or "bad?"

• *A teen decides to learn how to ski. Once on the slopes, she realizes that she is afraid of heights. Skiing down the mountain gives her a runaway, panicky feeling. Associating the experience with those feelings, she labels skiing "bad."*

As she grows and matures, she learns to enjoy adventure. She loves the feeling of being outdoors and decides to try skiing again. Skiing down the mountain gives her an exhilarating feeling of freedom. Now, she associates skiing with those feelings. She labels the experience "good."

Question: Is skiing "good" or "bad?"

• *Illusion says that positive and negative are separate. Reality explains that each explains one part of the same experience. When asked the question, "What is a forest?" the man in the first example can answer, "A forest is dark, dreary, and lonely. It can also be still, peaceful, and calm." Both the positive and negative experiences explain the reality of what a forest is, while the forest remains neutral.*

The carpenter can talk knowledgeably about being a carpenter. He knows both the positives and negatives. Both explain about being a carpenter.

The woman who now enjoys skiing can explain to a novice what to expect the first time on skis. She understands the full scope of a single experience. The experience of skiing remains neutral.

Positive And Negative Labels

Choose to eliminate the word "bad" from your vocabulary. Many feelings are associated with the word "bad" that lead to judgment and criticism of Self. Think in terms of "negative" qualities rather than "bad" qualities. Instead of labeling yourself "good" or "bad" merely acknowledge what does or does not exist within you. There is nothing wrong with negative. Negative is part of the process. Put it in its proper perspective to understand it for what it is.

Negative is not "bad." Negative promotes growth and prevents stagnation, often prompting you to move forward. Rich with learning, negative explains a part of God-Mind. **God-Mind is neither positive nor negative, but contains both.**

God-Mind provides all experience for you through your Oversoul. Give thanks for each one that comes your way. Learn from whatever is before you. Always remember that experience is neutral. It is your **reactions** that label experience either positive or negative.

Instead of quickly labeling an experience "negative," use some creative thinking. Circle around from the other side. Address it as a positive learning experience. As an objective observer, ask these questions:

What am I learning from this experience?

What weaknesses does it show me?

How can I strengthen my weaknesses?

What does it teach me about other people?

What does it teach me about life?

How will this experience make me a better or wiser person?

Your attitude changes when you take the time to answer these questions. Rather than resist the experience, flow with it. You may even find yourself enjoying the challenge of the situation rather than avoiding it. Your entire perception changes when you view difficult experiences as an opportunity for growth.

Positive is not better than negative. Each is equally necessary to understand the entire scope of a single experience. Throughout many lifelines, you experience a variety of negatives. Now it is time to maintain your balance by experiencing the positives.

Natural Process of Balance

There is a natural process of balance that maintains your identity as neutral energy. This means that every negative experience is balanced with a positive one, maintaining your neutral state. This can be described as follows:

$$(-1) \quad + \quad (+1) \quad = \quad 0$$
Negative Experience + Positive Experience = Neutral Experience

For every negative (-1) that is added to your list of experiences, a positive (+1) is added so that you always equal neutral (O). The examples given in the beginning of the chapter demonstrate balance within this lifeline. Because you have many lifelines, you may use several to attain balance for some of your experiences. The process of balance exists to help people understand the full spectrum of experience

Consider this. You have an unstable marriage (-1) in this lifeline. The natural process of balance applied says that eventually you will experience a stable marriage (+1). Your experiences teach you what marriage is (+ 1) and what marriage is not (-1). The experience of marriage remains neutral.

Sometimes you may give (+1) selflessly of yourself. Another time you take (-1) help. Giving and taking explain the full spectrum of one experience. Move through the illusion that negative is "bad." Negative is simply negative.

Interpersonal Bonds

The process of balance maintains bonds between one or more people. With agreement on the inner levels, these bonds allow each participant to understand the full spectrum of a single experience. Allan asks his friend Joe out to play. He shows Joe a wonderful tree that he just discovered. In his enthusiasm, Joe eagerly climbs the tree. He falls, breaking a leg. On the inner levels, both knew the result of this shared experience. Apparently, Joe needs this experience. Perhaps he is exploring the question: "What are legs?"

Two healthy legs explain legs. They answer the positive questions:
What is it like to have legs? What can I do with them?

A broken leg explains legs. Now, the negative question is answered:
What is it like without the use of legs? Joe now has full understanding of his original question, "What are legs?"

Allan chose to play a role that allowed Joe to answer his question. At some point in time, they may choose to reverse the roles. They both agree to the process of balance.

Examples Of Karmic Bonds

This process of balance exists among all life forms. You may hurt an animal in one lifeline. In another, that animal might be your treasured pet. Both experiences teach you about animals.

In one lifeline, you may choose an occupation that destroys the environment. In another, you may find the solution to prevent damage you caused. Both lifelines teach you about the environment.

Perhaps you have a lifeline filled with great respect for the Earth. You give (+ 1) respect. In another lifeline you are a prosperous farmer. You take (-1) the fruits of the Earth. This experience also teaches you about the environment.

You may have a lifeline where you are extremely poor, yet you share (+ 1) what you have with others. Perhaps in another lifeline you win the lottery. You give to others (+1), you take from others (-1). This teaches you about abundance.

Again, keep in mind that negative is not "bad." Negative is one side of a single experience. Always remember that the process of balance, exists for you.

Question Your Oversoul

Understanding that experience is neutral puts all experience in perspective. On some level of awareness you invite all experience into your life, including painful ones. All experience teaches you.

Whenever you experience something without understanding, question your Oversoul as an objective observer and listener. Ask for help to move through the illusion of "good" and "bad" into the reality that explains. You may receive satisfactory answers to some questions. To others, you may receive only partial answers. File partial answers away. Like the crossword puzzle, one day those partial answers will have meaning.

All experience promotes growth. Find out why you asked for a particular experience. Establish the learning that it brings. Then ask your Oversoul to build on that learning, taking you deeper inside of yourself.

ORGANIZE YOUR ENERGY

*"Organized energy increases your awareness of the
universal energy that flows up and down."*

With active lifestyles, it is important to organize personal, or psychic, energy. Organizing it in conscious awareness allows you to use it efficiently. Efficient use of psychic energy means you can increase the number of vertical experiences in each day. This means more answers on all levels of awareness.

Because you operate within the constraints of a twenty-four hour time period, your day only accommodates a given number of activities. A specified amount of time every day must be devoted to constants. Eating, sleeping, dressing, and personal hygiene are examples of constants. They cannot be eliminated, but you may be able to perform them more efficiently.

Evaluate Simple Tasks

Evaluate some of the simple tasks that you perform every day. Determine if they could be accomplished in a more efficient way. This does not mean rushing through tasks. Rather, it means performing the same task while expending less time, energy, and effort.

When preparing meals, for example, stop and think before you act. As an objective observer, evaluate the task. The following are samples of questions you might ask:

Do I need to make five trips to the refrigerator?
>   **or**
Can I accomplish the same thing in two trips?

Do I need to go into the pantry four times for four different ingredients?
>   **or**
Can I get everything in one trip?

Do I need to make one trip to the cabinet for dishes, one trip to a drawer for silverware, and one trip to another drawer for napkins?

or

Can I get everything out at once while standing in the same place?

Without rushing, you prepare the meal in a much more efficient way. You spend less psychic energy by taking the time to stop and think before you act. Every bit of energy saved gives you time and energy to spend elsewhere.

Saving energy throughout the day extends the twenty-four hour time period. Performing the same number of tasks in a more efficient way gives you "extra" time to add other experiences to the day. These might include walking, reading, relaxing, or completing unfinished projects. What activities would you add if you had "extra" time?

Most likely, thinking before you act will help you perform many daily tasks more efficiently while expending less energy. This continues to develop the creative thinking process. You perform ordinary tasks in extraordinary ways.

Body Tension Requires Energy

Think how much energy it takes to hold tension in the body. To illustrate this point, make a fist with your right hand. Squeeze it as hard as you can for sixty seconds. Your hand represents the tension that you hold in the body. After sixty seconds your hand is tired. You expend psychic energy to maintain tension. Releasing tension from the body adds to your pool of "extra" energy.

With your thoughts, feel and evaluate where you hold tension in the body. Squeeze your hand again to remember how tension feels. Now relax it so you know how relaxation feels. Release those feelings to your Oversoul.

Get in touch with every part of your body. Feel and release all tension. Begin at your feet, and slowly move up the lower legs, knees, upper legs, buttocks, lower back, middle back, upper back, shoulders, neck, head, upper arms, elbows, lower arms, and hands. When you find parts that hold tension, release that tension up to your Oversoul. Then relax that part. Make an effort to feel those parts a few times a day. Determine if they are in a state of tension or relaxation. Each time you release tension, you add to your "extra" energy pool. Use that "extra" energy for something constructive.

Think Before You Speak Or Act

Stop and think before you speak or act. Every time you choose to expend negative energy, you make the decision to give up positive energy. When you express hate, on some level you decide to give up love. When you express anxiety, you give up peace and calm. When you express harshness, you give up softness.

Whatever you express always returns. Negative energy going out means negative energy coming back. Hate going out means hate coming back. Anxiety going out means anxiety coming back. Harshness going out means harshness coming back. Be aware of the consequences of the actions that you choose.

Assume responsibility for your actions. Make conscious decisions of what and how you want to express. As an objective observer:

Observe yourself choose what and how you will express.

Observe yourself act out that expression.

Observe the effect of your actions on yourself, your environment, and others.

Act in conscious awareness. Be aware of both the positive and negative consequences of your actions at any given moment. When you choose to expend negative energy, observe yourself. As the objective observer, ask these questions:

How does this make me feel?

How does this make my body feel?

How does this make others feel?

How does this affect my environment?

Do I really want to act this way?

Am I ready to release this kind of expression, or some part of it, to my Oversoul?

Release all observations up to your Oversoul. Acknowledge responsibility for your actions. Also acknowledge your willingness to assume the consequences of those actions. Always keep in mind that consciously choosing to expend negative energy means giving up positive energy somewhere in your life.

Giving Energy To Others

On some level of awareness, you may choose to give your energy to others. This happens in a variety of ways. You may be giving physical, mental, emotional, spiritual, or even monetary support to someone who needs to be doing these things for him/herself. Often, people willingly hand over their responsibilities when given the choice.

You may provide an easy way for others to solve personal challenges. Instead of taking on their lessons, be a catalyst to help them grow by giving them tools. Remember, they need the satisfaction of solving their own challenges. They need the learning and growth that their challenges bring them. Always determine through the involved Oversouls who you need to help and how. When you help another without permission, you take away his/her lesson. In doing so, you develop a karmic bond that makes you responsible for that person's learning.

Choose Vertical Growth Activities

You always have many activities from which to choose. Do your best to choose the ones that promote vertical growth. Eliminate the ones that promote horizontal growth. You may belong to basketball, volleyball, and baseball teams. Are all three important? Maybe they are and maybe they are not. This is a choice only you can determine.

All activities are merely tools that teach you about yourself. Evaluate your activity by asking some of the following questions:

Does it—

lighten my life?

teach me to change?

develop my creative thinking process?

promote positive or negative growth?

teach me something that no other activity provides?

pull me up into my potential, keep me where I am, or pull me down?

Ask questions that are specific to your individual growth. Consciously decide what you want in your life and why. Giving up activities that you no longer need allows doors to open for new activities that match your current level of development.

Spend Meditation Time Wisely

Choose to spend your meditation time wisely. There is only a certain length of time available to devote to this level of deep inner concentration. Devote that time to accessing information that you need *right now*.

There are always many questions that you can ask your Oversoul, such as:

How can I read auras?

How can I have an out-of-body experience?

What is my future?

What are my other lifelines?

How did the universe begin?

For now, build your foundation. Concentrate on questions that specifically create inner harmony at this moment. Use the following questions as a guideline:

How can I change so my days flow smoother?

How can I improve my relationships?

What parts of myself am I ready to release?

How can I bring order into my life?

How can I communicate with others more effectively?

How can I move deeper into my center?

Taking the time to do this daily routine brings you into balance in a slow, methodical way. As that balance is achieved, the answers to the other questions will surface naturally.

Ask For Wisdom With Knowledge

Whenever you ask for knowledge, always ask for the wisdom to use it correctly. A child asking for power tools to create beautiful woodwork is asking for something beyond his skill level. He does not yet understand the accompanying responsibilities. Those potentially wonderful tools can do extensive damage without the wisdom to use them correctly. The child may seriously injure himself. Only after he hurts himself will he fully understand the consequences and his inability to use them properly. That may be of little comfort.

Like that child, your current scope of knowledge is limited. Whenever you ask for anything, **always** state that you only want whatever is in your best interest. Knowledge that you are not ready for may do more damage than good.

Do not wait until after-the-fact to understand why you were not given access to particular knowledge. Accept the wisdom of your Oversoul. Ask for knowledge that is pertinent to your immediate growth. Become strong and versatile in the present moment. When deeper truths are revealed to you, let it be through the natural process of unfoldment. Your Oversoul will always show you what you need to know. It is your responsibility to be open and receptive to the information. What you **want** to know and what you **need** to know can be very different. Trust your Oversoul to know what is best.

Make Specific Choices

Organizing your energy allows you to make specific choices quickly for extremely mundane activities. Shopping is a wonderful way to learn how efficient you can become. For instance, why touch several heads of lettuce before you choose the "right" one? Why not ask your Oversoul to direct you to "your" lettuce the first time?

A remodeling project may call for specific tools. Ask your Oversoul to direct you to the store with the best price on the item you need. Need an attorney? Look in the phone book. Ask your Oversoul to direct you to the best one for you. Allow yourself to find the most suitable person for the job the first time. Apply the same principle to all your activities. Apply it when you meet a new client, go on vacation, or clean your closets. All of this efficiency allows you to add to that "extra" energy pool that you are in the process of creating.

Use Universal Energy

Organized energy increases your awareness of the universal energy that flows up and down. Every time you stop and think before you act or speak, you send your thoughts up to your Oversoul. Then you wait for a feeling to come back down to you. Each time you move your psychic energy up instead of out, you allow your Oversoul to cleanse it and send it back to you on a new level of awareness.

When you do this, you apply basic metaphysical laws to basic activities. You do not do anything extraordinary, you simply use the laws. All it takes is a willingness to begin and **try**.

Start with simple tasks. Associate feelings of success with those simple tasks. Then work your way up to more complex activities. Learn the basics first. Realize that it takes time to build your foundation.

You are faced with dozens of ways to spend your energy every day. How you choose to organize and spend it is always your option. For example, you can—

perform your daily tasks efficiently or inefficiently.

maintain tension in your body or release it.

give your energy away or keep it.

express positive or negative energy.

ask questions out of curiosity or need during meditation.

work with your Oversoul or without it.

Whatever you decide, do so in awareness. Think before you speak or act, taking the time to evaluate the potential results of your decisions.

Organizing your energy allows room for more vertical experiences. This means more learning, growth, and eventually more inner knowledge and harmony.

DURING THE PROCESS

"Illusion tells you that you want to be the finished product. Reality tells you that there is no finished project. You are infinitely deep."

The tools and principles you are learning automatically move you into a deeper awareness of all that is real. The tools move you forward into your potential, giving guidance along the way. During the process, they instigate new inner activity.

This stirs up buried experiences, feelings, habit responses, vibratory imprints, knowledge, and lifelines. Because this changes the status quo, you move into unfamiliar territory. As with any change, you may feel uncomfortable at first. But as you move deeper, you also must move through these feelings of discomfort.

On one day, you feel good about moving in a new direction. The next, you feel depressed because you realize how much you are releasing. You may even feel empty when you release old habit responses and vibratory imprints that have been important for lifelines. You actually move into a type of death experience when you part with something that was very meaningful. As with any death, take time to adjust. Feel compassion for yourself as you move through the loss. Remember, you may always maintain contact with old parts of yourself through your Oversoul.

Whenever you feel empty inside, ask your Oversoul to fill up the empty spaces with:

Pink energy for love.
or
Blue energy for peace and calm.
or
Green energy for healing.

Release all that you feel up to your Oversoul.

Reality explains that all these feelings exist to move you into the final stage of the releasing process. Old vibratory imprints **try** to pull you back. New vibratory imprints grow stronger, **trying** to pull you into them. At this point, you finally release old habit responses and vibratory imprints. You automatically move into the **being** stage.

At times when you **try** to move forward, you may feel like you are standing still. You may feel restless because you are unable to detect inner growth. As long as you try, be assured that something, somewhere is stirring around.

Progress In A Methodical Manner

Because these tools and principles help you progress in a methodical, balanced manner, you may not always be easy to identify specific growth. As a child, you were not consciously aware when your physical body grew. Yet, it still grew. One arm did not suddenly become six inches longer than the other. One foot did not suddenly require a much larger shoe than the other foot. Every part of your physical body grew in direct proportion to every other part.

In the same way, you progress in a methodical, balanced manner on many levels of awareness. Your conscious, subconscious, and superconscious minds all work together to maintain a state of inner balance. These minds often work at the same time on different subjects.

As further explanation, think about a time when you were driving. Suddenly, you arrive at your destination. You realize that you were daydreaming, and cannot actually remember driving the car. What part of your mind drove the car without getting you killed? What part of your mind was wandering? Two parts of your mind functioned at the same time, each on different subjects, each on different levels. As you continue to bring more knowledge forward into your conscious mind, you become aware of the three minds working together.

Bring The Body Into Balance

The body is only a home for the real you. But, it is vital that it receive proper care to allow you to reach optimum mental and spiritual levels. This is necessary for you to express new knowledge. Therefore, as your mental and spiritual food changes, the physical food you give your body must also change. This allows the body to continue balancing itself with the mind and spirit.

The food your body craves may automatically change as you change. The food that you put into the body is symbolic of the food that you put into your mind. By listening to the body, you can help it make the necessary adjustments in conscious awareness.

When the body is hungry, ask it what it **needs**. Then use the listening skills that you are acquiring, and pay attention. Separate the **wants** of the taste buds from the **needs** of the body. It is possible to satisfy the **wants** of the taste buds, without satisfying the **needs** of the body.

The stomach and intestinal tract can be full while the body is hungry for specific nutrients. This means that you continually feed it more than it needs, while it tries to extract nutrients that simply are not there. The end result is extra unwanted weight.

Pay attention to how the body feels after eating various foods. Feel what makes it strong and healthy, and what makes it weak. Listening through your Oversoul, communicate with it by asking specific questions. Ask it if it wants:

Protein—red meat, meat, seafood, nuts, dairy products.

Vegetables—green, yellow; cooked, raw.

Fruits—citrus, bananas, apples; cooked, raw.

Grain—wheat, oats, barley, millet; bread; crackers; cooked or cold.

Dairy products—milk, cheese, yogurt.

As you eat, ask the body to tell you when it is full. The **taste buds** may want more food, but the **body** may be satisfied.

Sometimes, the body may require foods that you think are unhealthy for it. White sugar, for example, may irritate the nerves, but for some people it helps to ground them. If this is the case, determine how much white sugar is **needed**, not **wanted**, and stop there. Salt may irritate the blood veins, but it also cuts mucus in the body. Pay attention to what the body needs, for whatever reason.

Changing your diet too quickly may throw the body into a "healing crisis." Simply put, it can become sick. Just as a drug addict suffers withdrawal symptoms, the body may suffer withdrawal symptoms from certain types of foods, specifically:

White sugar.

White flour.

Salt.

Flesh foods.

Processed foods.

Alcohol.

Chemicals and preservatives.

Any time you decide to change your diet, take a few minutes to explain the new plan to your body. Ask its cooperation, and thank it for its help.

Eliminate unnecessary foods from your diet by gradually reducing the intake. This puts less stress on the body, decreasing the possibility of a "healing crisis." Sometimes, you may get sick anyway. This only means that old toxins from unnecessary vibratory imprints are on their way out of the body. Instead of becoming discouraged, merely send them on up to your Oversoul. Thank them for the learning they brought you. Continue to ask the body to teach you how to strengthen it. If you take the time to listen, it will instruct you.

Moving Through The Layers

The tools that you are acquiring move you through many layers of experience. Each layer contains a part of the one on top of it. For instance, each one contains some resentment, fear, guilt, low Self-esteem, as well as some contentment, courage, harmony, high Self-esteem.

As you move through one layer, you feel good because you think all resentment is released. Then when you least expect it, resentment shows up again. You wonder where it came from. You thought you released it from your life.

You merely touch into the next layer. Then you move through resentment again. Finally, when you think that it is gone, it shows up again. Because you are tired of moving through resentment, this may disappoint you.

You like the thrill of learning new principles, applying them, and having immediate results. Now you have to dig a little deeper. You may have to wait a little longer for results as you move into deeper areas of yourself.

Clean

When you feel really stuck cleaning is a simple activity that may get you moving again. Discarding old, unnecessary possessions is symbolic of discarding old, unnecessary habit responses and vibratory imprints. The outer always reflects the inner. This is a law. An outer change anywhere automatically changes something inside.

You do not have to start a major cleaning campaign. Clean out your briefcase, a drawer in your desk, a shelf in your closet. Pull a few weeds, rake some leaves, plant flowers. Paint or redecorate. Wash a window or two. Dispose of anything that you no longer need or appreciate. Any cleaning, anywhere prompts change.

Walk

Walking also helps move you. Walking brings the physical body into balance. When the body shifts, mind and spirit also shift, because all are interconnected. This, too, is a law. Balancing the body helps create the shift that brings *you* into balance.

As you walk hang your arms at your side. Allow them to swing freely, without burdening them with packages, briefcases, or shoulder bags. Be aware of the shift in body weight from left to right, and right to left. You may walk many miles before the corresponding mental and spiritual shifts occur. When these shifts occur, new avenues of action become apparent.

Sleep

Sleeping patterns sometimes change during the process of inner growth. You may suddenly need more or less sleep. Buried turbulence may rise up into your conscious mind during the night, resulting in nightmares and/or bad dreams. Review and release these dreams up to your Oversoul.

Holding Patterns

Your growth may move into a holding pattern while waiting for other players to move into position. Others also have lessons to complete. They must develop the necessary requirements to move into your life. When everyone is ready, the next act begins.

Ask Your Oversoul Questions

Whenever you want to move but are not sure how, remember to ask your Oversoul questions. Your Oversoul depends on you for feedback. You are now a partner in the growth process. Your questions help your Oversoul determine your strengths and weaknesses, and how to correctly move you.

Learn to interpret the responses from your Oversoul. Sometimes it is difficult to feel the response of your Oversoul because it is easy to stop in the space above your head that contains your own thoughts. Remember to push your thoughts up high enough to connect with your Oversoul. Eventually, you recognize the specific feeling when you make the connection.

Remember, you are in the process of learning Oversoul communication. You do not have perfect Oversoul communication yet. Compare yourself to children learning to walk. Only practice teaches them to walk, but eventually the children **will** walk.

Incorrect Movement

Rather than move incorrectly, you may make a conscious decision to do nothing at all. Fear and ego may tell you to stand still, rather than risk making a mistake. Moving incorrectly for any situation is not "wrong," it merely indicates to your Oversoul where you need guidance.

Your Oversoul then brings that part of yourself into balance. The first step in change is to **try**. As long as you **try**, you will be guided.

If you choose to stand still, your Oversoul will try to get you to move. This may be in the form of a negative learning experience because you know how to react to the negative. This gives you a chance to move, even though it is through your "old" learning process.

If you continue to ignore the negative learning experience, you will stagnate. Your Oversoul then has the option of removing you from the physical body. It can choose to place you into a new situation, where you have no choice but to move. When in doubt, always remember:

Incorrect movement is better than no movement at all.

Keep Moving Forward

Recognizing the progress that you make toward inner awareness is wonderful. You acknowledge where you were and where you are now. Sometimes you become so appreciative of your growth that you reach a plateau. The present looks so good in comparison to the past that you let illusion tell you that life cannot get any better. So you decide to stop growing.

When you believe illusion, you let go of the momentum that keeps you moving forward. Always remember that behind unopened doors are experiences and knowledge waiting for you to enter. Reality explains that your growth is still in progress. Enjoy and appreciate where you are. But allow your past to be part of the motivating force that continues to propel you into your potential.

Appreciate The Present

As doors begin to open, you start to realize your potential. This may make you dissatisfied and impatient with the present. You may even allow bitterness to creep in as you wish to be "there" instead of "here."

Completion of current lessons is necessary to be strong enough to claim your potential when the time is right. Illusion tells you that you want to be the finished product. Reality explains that there is no finished product. You always grow. You are infinitely deep. Your journey is forever.

You are here to enjoy each period of transition—

From the beginning...
                   through the middle...
                                        onto the end.

Then you go onto the next experience, and the next, and the next. You only exist for experience.

BLENDING IT ALL TOGETHER

"Everything is equal importance."

Once there was a businessman with a successful business, a beautiful family, and a supportive network of friends. Yet, he still felt emptiness inside. He longed to know more about God-Mind and the mysteries of life. His constant prayer to God-Mind was, "Teach me about you. Teach me about who and what you are."

One day while meditating he was shown a lifeline during which he was a monk living in a monastery. He lived a cloistered life with ample time for contemplation and meditation. His constant prayer to God-Mind was, "Teach me about you. Teach me about who and what you are."

In that lifeline God-Mind answered him and said, "I will teach you about me. I will teach you about who and what I am. I will give you a lifeline with a successful business, a beautiful family, and a supportive network of friends. This will help to explain who and what I am. "

All That Is comes Out Of God-Mind

Illusion tells you that God-Mind is separate from the outer material world. Reality explains that it is all the same. The division of spiritual versus non-spiritual functions is only an illusion of human thought.

This world is created by God-Mind. All that exists is a part of God-Mind. All that exists has a purpose. When you do not understand that purpose, you may label a certain activity "nonspiritual" or even "bad."

In effect, this is a judgment and criticism of God-Mind's world. With your Oversoul and God-Mind, you create the very small role that you play. However, only God-Mind creates the overall drama. As you release the need to judge Self, the need to judge the outer world decreases. Remember, the outer always reflects the inner and vice versa.

As with Self, learn to accept what is. As an objective observer ask your Oversoul and God-Mind to explain the purpose of what exists. Send your questions up through your own thoughts to your Oversoul. Wait for the answers to come back down the channel. If you do not receive any explanation, continue to send your questions up. When you are ready the answers will come to you.

Instead of trying to invoke your will upon creation, allow creation to be. This acceptance and understanding automatically moves you vertically. From this new position, you see the big picture more clearly.

As an example, remember that there are Oversouls for all of creation. There are Oversouls for the mineral, plant, and animal kingdoms, as well as humankind. Each kingdom is in the process of experiencing God-Mind. So in turn, a car is merely part of the mineral kingdom in the process of experiencing. A car answers many questions for God-Mind about what the mineral kingdom is and is not.

Illusion says that you own the car. Reality explains that you are only together through mutual agreement. When the car is through with you, it will be sold, wrecked, or fall apart.

Cars help answer the question, "What is the mineral kingdom?" Cars have an important part in the play. They challenge humankind to bring untapped knowledge forward into the collective conscious mind. That knowledge is needed to move into the next level of transportation. As a part of God-Mind, cars deserve respect.

All that exists deserves respect for the part that it plays in the overall drama. Respect for Self is reflected by respect for the outer world. Consider some of the following areas that illusion labels "non-spiritual."

Money

Illusion often labels money "non-spiritual." Reality explains that money is as spiritual as prayer and meditation. They both originate from God-Mind. Money is a neutral medium of exchange that allows experience, and represents expended energy.

A ship builder exchanges the intangible energy spent building a ship for a tangible representation of that energy. That tangible representation is called "money," and represents the expended energy. Money creates a balancing cycle of energy going out, energy coming in.

The exchange of money for goods and services continues the balancing cycle. Someone expends intangible energy to create goods and services. In turn, he/she is given a tangible representation.

Money also simplifies. Without money, the world would operate entirely on a barter system. In many instances that is acceptable. But what if you are a dentist? You may want some apples from the orchardist down the road. He may not need any dental work in exchange. In a moneyless system even a simple task such as getting apples may become complex.

Redefining money puts it into proper perspective. The outer world always reflects the inner world. Money is symbolic of energy. Lack of enough money to meet your needs is a form of Self-denial. In a way this says, "I am not worthy of receiving the equivalent of my energy expenditure." If this is the case, use the following affirmations as new seed thoughts:

I release the need for lack.

I am worthy of money.

I accept money as a part of God-Mind's world.

I deserve to experience God-Mind's abundant supply of energy.

Accepting money into your life acknowledges that God-Mind provides enough energy for you to comfortably experience the outer world.

Your Body

Illusion often labels your body "non-spiritual." Reality explains that your body is part of the process. You are not the body, but you operate in and through it. Your body is an instrument that is refined daily with thoughts and actions as well as diet and exercise. Fine-tuning the instrument that is provided for you ensures efficient communication between yourself, your Oversoul, and God-Mind.

Anytime that you judge or criticize your body, you dissipate the psychic energy that maintains it. This accelerates physical aging and deterioration. Instead, evaluate your body. Set a goal to improve it.

Because your body is not sick does not mean that it is healthy. Ask for guidance to create health within it through thought, actions, diet, and exercise. Ask it what it needs to maintain health.

Communicate with it. When you listen to it you may be surprised at what you learn. Offer it to your Oversoul and God-Mind. Ask that it be blessed and loved. Use the following affirmations as new seed thoughts:

I release the need to judge and criticize my body.

I love and appreciate my body.

I listen to my body and allow it to teach me.

I ask my Oversoul and God-Mind to bless and love my body.

Go beyond accepting your body. Take the time to love and appreciate it. Thank it for working with you.

Play And Rest

Illusion often says that play and rest are "non-spiritual" activities. Reality explains that play and rest create balance. Together they help you:

break up patterns that are too serious and intense.

lighten your attitudes.

become more flexible.

develop distance from your everyday routine.

view life as an objective observer.

quiet and calm your conscious mind.

replenish the psychic energy of your body.

Above all, play and rest allow the mind and body to relax. Tension causes blood veins to constrict. This decreases the flow of blood carrying essential oxygen to the brain and other vital organs. As a result, the mind and body function less efficiently. Spiritual growth slows when the necessary instrument (your body) does not function at optimum capacity.

In a relaxed state, blood flows more freely throughout the body. Psychic energy circulates through the body with less restraint. Efficient functioning of the physical body increases mental capacity. In response, spiritual growth accelerates.

When you "let go, you let God-Mind," as the saying goes. Play and rest help you let go. In a relaxed state, inner communication comes forward into your conscious mind. How many times have you struggled at length through an activity with unsuccessful results? Usually, the answer comes to you not long after you give up and walk away. You finally "let go."

Play and rest are productive activities essential to physical, mental, and spiritual growth. Use the following affirmations as new seed thoughts:

I deserve to play and rest.

I deserve balance in my life.

I allow myself to relax.

I "let go and let God-Mind."

Everything produced in the outer world originates from the inner world. Play and rest help to establish the pathway that takes you within.

Occupation

Illusion may label your occupation as a "non-spiritual" activity. Reality explains that all activity is spiritual. Everything that you do, you do for God-Mind. If you are a minister, the outer world labels your occupation "spiritual." If you work on an assembly line, it is up to you to label your occupation "spiritual." In other words, this gives you the responsibility to identify yourself. Your identity now comes from within instead of from the outer world.

Occupations always reflect the present. Your occupation teaches you when you let it. Your occupation may allow you to expend physical energy to drain inner anger. Your occupation may help you to move through fear. Or, it may keep you in fear. Service occupations may allow you to balance past actions through present activities—if, in the past you "took" (-1), now you "give" (+1).

Occupations also acknowledge acquired skills from all lifelines. Lifelines travel in cycles. Your occupation is a key to who you are and the experiences that brought you to this point in time.

To better understand your occupation, use the following affirmations as new seed thoughts:

I recognize that all activity is spiritual.

I offer my work to my Oversoul and God-Mind.

I allow my occupation to teach me about my present.

I allow my occupation to teach me about my past.

Your occupation provides a wonderful opportunity for you to blend inner and outer activity.

Redefine Life

Redefine any part of life that you criticize or judge because it is "non-spiritual." Remember that any outer criticism or judgment is only a reflection of inner criticism or judgment. As you accept Self as is, you accept the outer world as is.

Acceptance of Self leads to respect for the part of God-Mind that you are. In turn, you respect the outer world for the part of God-Mind that it is. Continue to evaluate all activity, releasing to your Oversoul what you no longer need. Then move forward into the next experience, always remembering that—

Everything is equal in importance.

Everything is spiritual.

Everything exists for God-Mind.

SPIRITUALITY SURROUNDS YOU

*"Illusion taught you to separate. Reality explains that
everything is one and the same."*

Spirituality is a moment-by-moment daily occurrence. Every moment is a function of God-Mind. Each one is equally meaningful. One is not more or less spiritual than another. Illusion may tell you to go out in search of spirituality. Reality explains that all you have to do is remain in your center and accept what is already yours. Spirituality is a state of inner being.

Each moment in your life reflects your state of inner being. Whatever you choose to put in your moments defines your personal spirituality. How you treat yourself, others, and the outer world reflects your state of inner being.

Spirituality is private and personal. You do not need to tell or show others how spiritual you are. The more that you accomplish on the inner levels, the cleaner and clearer you stay. You teach others simply by **being.** On some level of awareness they notice that your body, mind, and spirit express something "different ":

Your body is relaxed.

Your words are clear.

Your surrounding space is clean.

You listen and observe objectively.

Your energy moves vertically instead of horizontally.

Your energy is gathered in one place and is strong and solid.

You have respect for Self, others, and the outer world.

You are noticed just because. There is no ego involved, or any outer expression of inner devotion. You just are.

Spirituality Is Comfortable

As you discover and define your own inner state of being, you find that spirituality encompasses your life in a natural, comfortable way. Your inner world easily integrates with the outer world. You find that all your activities easily meld into a single expression of spirituality.

This process acknowledges what already exists. The difference is that you now allow everything to be a part of you. Illusion taught you to separate. Reality explains that everything is one and the same. Everything answers the questions:

Who am I?

What am I?

Who is God-Mind?

What is God-Mind?

Spirituality surrounds you; it has always been there; it will always be there. Acknowledge and accept what is already yours.

THE KNOWLEDGE IS YOURS

*"The speed and depth of your personal
growth is up to you."*

Everything takes practice, including moving deeper inside of yourself. The knowledge is fascinating, the process endless. Each time you establish and understand one set of knowledge, the next set automatically reveals itself.

What was once mysterious and secretive is now simple, orderly, and explicable. Knowledge that explains the inner world also explains the outer, and vice versa. You see your life simplify as a result of applying that knowledge.

Practice, Practice, Practice!

The knowledge is in place waiting for you to "discover." The next step is yours. The speed and depth of your personal growth is up to you. Are you willing to:
keep an open mind?
let go of the old?
look at yourself with honesty?
try new methods and techniques?
practice, practice, practice?

Anyone who is an expert on anything has undoubtedly spent numerous hours studying the subject. That is how one becomes an expert: ask questions, test theories, and practice, practice, practice!

New techniques and methods in any field require practice. Personal growth is no different. The degree of expertise you develop depends upon the time and intensity that you wish to devote to yourself. How important *are* you?

Understand Your Own Microcosmic Mystery

This section of the book establishes growth possibilities, along with tools and techniques for taking yourself there. With time and practice, understand your own microcosmic mystery by:

establishing a goal of vertical growth.

observing and listening objectively.

learning how to change.

identifying and releasing old, unnecessary habit responses.

moving through illusion into reality.

understanding the neutrality of experience.

organizing your psychic energy.

taking care of body, mind, and spirit.

respecting yourself and the outer world.

Each subject area listed above probably has more answers than you have questions. This means that each is ripe for exploration. Decide for yourself how deep you want to explore and the time you want to devote. But whatever your decision, make it in conscious awareness.

Your Path Is In Place

As you leave behind old behavior patterns and ways of thinking, appreciate the experiences and lessons that they brought. Your path is in place, waiting to be utilized. You already stand upon it. Continue moving forward as it becomes clearer and more accessible. Enjoy the freedom that comes from "Moving Forward"!

APPENDICES II

SOME THINGS TO TRY

OBSERVE

Observe your body language.

At what point in conversations does it change?

Does your body express itself differently with different people?

Observe the colors that you choose to wear.

Do you wear some colors more than others?

Does one color make you feel different than another color?

Do you choose specific colors for specific occasions?

Observe the people that you choose around yourself.

What do they teach you about yourself?

What specific reactions do specific people bring out in you?

LISTEN

Listen to your words.

Do they affirm the positive or negative in your life?

Listen to the tone of your voice.

Do you like what you hear?

Listen to the feelings behind your words.

Do your words match your feelings?

Listen to the energy behind your words.

Do you like the feeling of the energy?

Listen to the colors that you use when you speak.

What do they tell you about yourself?

When you are quiet, listen to the vibrations around yourself.

What secrets do they share about your state of inner being?

RELEASE JUDGMENT AND CRITICISM OF SELF

Choose to replace the word "bad" with the word "negative."

As you observe and evaluate inner qualities, think in terms of "positive" and "negative."

Observe your feelings to determine if this makes you feel less judgmental and critical of yourself.

CHANGE

Do three ordinary tasks in an extraordinary way.
Decide if you want to do this for a day, a week, or even a month.
Write these down. Then observe how you feel.

Did you successfully accomplish these small changes?

Did you feel enjoyment or stress?

If you felt awkward, was it okay that you felt awkward?

Did these small changes help open the creative thinking process?

Is change easy, difficult, or somewhere between for you?

Does making these small changes affect your ability to implement larger, more significant change?

HABIT RESPONSES

What situations and/or people always evoke the same reactions from you?

Do you like these reactions?

If not, how would you like to respond?

Resolve to stop and think before you act the next time.

Give yourself credit even if you stop and think after the fact.

Acknowledge any progress you make, regardless of how insignificant it may seem.

SPEND YOURSELF WISELY

Choose three simple tasks.

Determine how to perform them more efficiently.

Try the new way.

Evaluate your feelings.

Does performing them more efficiently add to your energy pool?

How would you use "extra" energy if you had it?

Are there other tasks that might be performed more efficiently?

CLEAN YOUR HOME

Choose something in your home or workplace that needs cleaning.
Set a goal that is obtainable even if it is one drawer or half of a closet.
After you clean it, observe how you feel.

Does it make you feel good to get it in order?

Did getting rid of unnecessary items make your mental house feel lighter or emptier, or both?

Do you somehow feel cleaned out?

WHAT DO YOU LIKE ABOUT YOURSELF?

Make a list of ten qualities or traits that you like about yourself.

Is this easy or difficult?

Always take time to appreciate who you are and what you have accomplished.

AFFIRMATIONS

Choose one or two of the following affirmations. Make any changes that personalize them for you. Think, say, or write them throughout your day. The more you utilize them, the faster they will move you.

BALANCING THE BODY
I release the need for excess weight.
I release the need for food that is unhealthy for my body.
I deserve to have a healthy body.
I listen to my body.
I release the need for body tension.
My body is relaxed and at peace.
I easily separate the needs from the wants of my body.

CENTERING
I breathe myself into my center.
My center is strong and flexible.
I remain centered and calm.
I remain centered and calm in the midst of outer confusion/turmoil.
I touch into the peace within.
I observe myself from my center.
I remain in my center as the objective observer.
My center provides a safe, comfortable place from which to observe.
I feel one with myself, my Oversoul, and God-Mind while in my center.

CHANGE
I move through my fear of the unknown.
I am comfortable in the midst of my discomfort.
I am willing to release the old.
I easily accept and implement the new.
I am flexible.
Change is possible.
Change is acceptable.
I enjoy the challenge of change.

HABIT RESPONSES
I release the need for all old, unnecessary habit responses.
I choose my own actions and reactions.
I always have a choice.
I stop and think before I react.
I assume responsibility for my thoughts, words, and deeds.
I choose habit responses that recreate my life in a positive way.

ILLUSION

I release the illusion of who I am.
I accept the reality of who I am.
I expand my definition of Self.
I accept reality in exchange for illusion.
I penetrate the layers of illusion.
I release Self-imposed limitations.
I release memories that keep me in illusion.
I move through and beyond illusion.
I allow reality to explain.

KNOWLEDGE

I move forward into "new" knowledge.
I ask for the wisdom to use all knowledge correctly.
I accept responsibility for deeper inner knowledge.

OBJECTIVE LISTENING

I objectively listen to myself.
I release words that weaken body, mind, or spirit.
I choose words that affirm the positive in my life.
I match feelings with words.
I listen through my Oversoul.
I am open and receptive to all levels of listening.
I move into continually deeper levels of inner listening.

OBJECTIVE OBSERVING

I observe myself in conscious awareness.
I observe myself without judgment or criticism.
I release the need to judge and criticize Self.
I release the parts of myself that I no longer need.
I appreciate who I am and the learning that brought me here.
I am honest with myself.
I accept myself exactly as I am.
I respect myself.
I release the need to judge and criticize the outer world.
I accept the outer world as is.
I ask my Oversoul to explain the outer world.
I respect the outer world.

SPENDING ENERGY

I organize my energy in conscious awareness.
I spend my energy efficiently.
I stop and think before I speak or act.
I use universal energy to make specific choices quickly.

VERTICAL EXPERIENCES

I release the need for horizontal experiences.
I choose vertical experiences.
I choose vertical experiences to accelerate my inner growth.
I move my psychic energy up instead of out.
I extract all knowledge available from every experience.
I allow vertical experiences to move me through illusion.

MEDITATIONS

MOVE DEEP WITHIN YOUR CENTER

Follow your breath deep within your center.

With each breath in, silently say "deeper."

With each breath out, silently say "deeper."

Feel yourself sink into continually deeper levels of silence.

Feel the peace and comfort that exists within the depths of your being.

Recognize that you feel safe and secure within your center.

Feel the connection that already exists between you, your Oversoul, and God-Mind.

Recognize that their strength is your strength.

Know that as long as you remain in your center, you can observe whatever you need to observe without discomfort.

In the same way, know that the turbulence of the outer world can circulate all around you without pulling you into it as long as you remain in your center.

Release all your feelings up to your Oversoul. Give thanks for the knowledge.

LISTEN TO YOUR VIBRATORY IMPRINTS

Ask your Oversoul to help you listen to the experiences that your vibratory imprints contain.

Follow your breath deep within.

With every breath, feel yourself sink deeper and deeper within.

Feel the inner connection between yourself, your Oversoul, and God-Mind.

Listen.

Do not expect anything; allow whatever happens to happen.

MEDITATION FOR CHANGE

As you follow your breath deep within, state the following to your Oversoul and God-Mind:

Thank you for all that I have and all that I receive. Thank you for all my challenges. I accept them as the learning tools that they are. I only ask that you explain them so that I can understand the learning that they bring. For this reason, I offer them back to you.

I am willing to release them to you permanently so that I may grow into new avenues of awareness. I am willing to explore any options that you present. I am willing to accept any people or challenges that you choose to put before me. I only ask that you explain so that I may understand.

(Remain in your center. Listen to the silence.)

For this learning and the knowledge that it contains, I give thanks.

RELEASING MEDITATION

Without labeling specific areas, ask that all unnecessary patterns, habit responses, and vibratory imprints be released from your life. Breathe in the new from your Oversoul through the top of your head to the base of your spine. Observe that it is clear and clean.

Breathing out in reverse order, release the old. Observe that it is dark and heavy. When you are through, observe how you feel. Release those feelings up to your Oversoul. Give thanks for the releasing process.

RELEASING HABIT RESPONSES

Your habit responses are interconnected. Deciding to change one instigates a chain reaction in many areas. In conscious awareness, determine those areas to accelerate the change.

For example, you decide that irritation is a habit response. Ask your Oversoul to show you all the places in your life where irritation exists. Release those feelings up to your Oversoul. Continue to trace irritation feelings back through your life as far as possible.

Every time you release those feelings, the vibratory imprint that holds the habit response of irritation weakens. Eventually, you will notice that the outer world irritates you less. The uncomfortable feelings that lived within took up space. Releasing them allows room for comfortable feelings to exist.

RELEASING UNCOMPLETED EXPERIENCES

Choose a lingering experience that you would like to "forget."

Breathe yourself into your center.

As an objective observer, allow the experience to rise before your inner eye.

Observe the emotions that you feel. Allow the part of you that contains those emotions to yell, scream, cry, or do whatever it needs for release.

Observe this part of yourself expressing to your Oversoul exactly how it feels. Ask your Oversoul to pass this message on to all involved individuals via their Oversouls.

Release everything up to your Oversoul as it occurs. Acknowledge your learning from the experience. Observe how you feel after releasing it. Give thanks for the experience and complete your meditation.

MEDITATION FOR INNER HARMONY

State the following to your Oversoul and God-Mind:

Thank you for all the tools that you give me to help me learn and grow. All I have to do is breathe myself into my center and you are there. Acknowledging your strength acknowledges my strength. Remaining in my center, I feel and understand your vastness. At the same time, I understand my own vastness.

As with you, I understand that I am neither positive nor negative, but contain both. I know that each explains a part of myself. And every part of me exists for a purpose. As I release the turbulent parts with understanding, I move closer to the peaceful parts. In the end, they are all one and the same. They are all a part of me, and all a part of you.

I am discovering that I like myself. I like who and what I am. I appreciate the experiences that brought me to this point in time. And better still, I understand these experiences. Moving through the illusion of turbulence takes me into the reality of the deep inner peace which already exists within. All I have to do is to let go and let God-Mind.

For this knowledge and these experiences, I give thanks.

MEDITATION REVIEW

Take a few moments to review your meditation time. Breathe yourself into your center and evaluate your accomplishments. Use the following questions as a guideline:

Is your meditation time worthwhile?

What are you accomplishing?

Is your body more relaxed than when you first began?

Does your breathing pull you into your center?

Are you moving into deeper levels of inner awareness?

Are you touching into a place of inner peace?

Are you cultivating skills that you can use throughout the day?

Are you able to observe and listen to yourself objectively?

Are you less judgmental and critical of yourself?

Are you finding out who you are?

Compared to when you first started meditating, where are you now?

SECTION III
FINDING THE BALANCE

FINDING THE BALANCE

"Respect for the process of balance develops patience."

You probably think of yourself as "one." Most people do. One body, one person. Your one body, however, is made up of millions of cells. **You** are the result of hundreds of experiences. And every experience is comprised of many, many different emotions.

These different emotions organize themselves into specific groups within your auric field. For instance, all anger emotions gather into one group, all compassion emotions gather into one group, and so on. Each group is a part of the overall personality that you choose to express in this lifeline.

These groups circle around the nucleus that is you. They function side by side, day by day. Each group is in a constant state of adjustment depending upon which one needs to fulfill a particular role at a specific time.

When you wish to express anger, you call upon the group of emotions containing anger. The anger group swells up, taking its place front and center. While you stand quietly by, this part of Self proudly displays its talents. The other groups shrink into the background to keep the balance within.

When you call upon the compassion group, the anger group agrees to retreat. Although it still exists, it remains silent while the compassion group expresses. These tradeoffs occur automatically every second of every day.

Who Has The Power?

As long as you remain in your center, **you** maintain inner power by calling upon these groups of emotions as needed. However, these groups can become extremely strong, eventually developing a consciousness of their own. When this occurs, they are no longer simply a group of emotions. They are now legitimate "sub-personalities." These sub-personalities continue to circle around the nucleus that is you.

As these sub-personalities gather strength, they sometimes try to gain control over the nucleus that contains the real you. When you least expect it, they push you out of your central command position and take control. For example, driving down the highway without a care in the world, the car on your left suddenly cuts in front of you. Taken by surprise, your guard goes down. The anger group, now a strong sub-personality named "Anger," sees its chance. Anger slips through this window of opportunity, and voila! Anger has control of you, the situation, and perhaps the rest of your day—how exciting for Anger!

Positive sub-personalities also try to gain control. Consider Compassion, as an example. You are now a purchasing agent for a small company. A salesman whom you have never met before comes into your office with a new product. The product does not impress you, but the salesman does. As he gives his best sales pitch, your attention wanders to the wedding ring on his finger.

You wonder if he has a family, house payments, bills. As your mind drifts, your guard goes down. Compassion sees its opportunity. The next thing you know, a completed purchase order is in your hand. The salesman is gone. Now all you have to do is explain the purchase to your employer.

When only one sub-personality takes control, it is often easy to identify. When several sub-personalities fight for control, recognition becomes more difficult. For instance, a good friend betrays a confidence. Anger is now joined by Hurt, as well as a variety of other sub-personalities. Each sub-personality tells you a different emotional story about this one situation. As you stand in the center listening to them all, you recognize that you have a difficult decision. Do you continue or terminate the friendship? An inner tug-of-war commences.

You are no longer in balance as all the sub-personalities vie for your attention. Each one wants to take control of the situation. Each one has its own identity and strength. Each one pulls on the nucleus that is you. Which one will you listen to? Will it be: Anger, Hurt, Judgment, Criticism, Distrust, Loneliness, Trust, Understanding, Forgiveness, or Compassion?

If you decide to allow Forgiveness to rule the situation, how do you explain this to Anger? Or to Distrust? Or to Judgment and Criticism? Your friendship can only exist in comfort when every sub-personality agrees to support the decision that you make.

All sub-personalities must be sorted, labeled, and addressed to restore some sort of inner comfort. All negative and positive sub-personalities must equal zero in the final equation. This means that the overall feeling of the combined sub-personalities must be neutral for you to finally feel peace within.

A Giant Amoeba

Compare yourself to a giant amoeba. An amoeba is a one-celled animal with protrusions all over itself similar to arms. In order to move, the amoeba must get all the protrusions going in the same direction at the same time.

You are like the amoeba. Each protrusion contains a sub-personality. When you decide to move in any direction, all these sub-personalities must move with you. Without their cooperation, this can be nearly impossible.

Sometimes the more determined you are to move in a particular direction, the stronger the opposite pull. There are sub-personalities that simply do not want to go. As soon as you stop trying, the obstinate ones take the opportunity to anchor themselves firmly in the status quo. Moving in one direction takes concentrated effort. All protrusions must be addressed so that the entire organism can move forward.

The Positive Purpose Of Negative Pull

Believe it or not, negative pull does have a positive purpose. This pull maintains inner balance. Anger helps you to remember the incident. Distrust teaches you to think before you speak. Judgment and Criticism force you to acknowledge your friend's weaknesses. The inner tug-of-war continues as facts are evaluated. The positives and negatives help maintain inner balance.

Creating A "New" Self

These sub-personalities are actually in the process of integrating into one distinct personality. You are in a continual process of creating a "new" self. You have a personality that allows you to be a specific character in a particular play. This inner tug-of-war creates a new personality that allows you to read from a new script. Your thoughts, words, and actions mold and shape this new self.

As you grow and change, you make continual conscious and unconscious decisions about this new personality. By consciously acknowledging all involved sub-personalities, you identify the ones that need to be strengthened as well as the ones that need to be weakened.

Perhaps, for example, your lifeline companion has a stubborn streak. The only time that he/she really pays attention to your needs is when you are angry. You realize the importance of Anger, so you continually strengthen Anger. The detriment of keeping Anger strong for this role is that Anger sometimes slips out at inopportune times.

One day, your companion enrolls in a self-improvement course. He/she realizes that the stubbornness has got to go. Because of his/her change, you no longer need such a strong Anger sub-personality. You can consciously choose to weaken that sub-personality to match your changing role. He/she no longer needs your Anger to get his/her attention.

You decide to relate to your companion with Compassion rather than Anger. To do so, you release the strength of Anger as you increase the strength of Compassion. Strengthening Compassion for this relationship creates a stronger Compassion for other areas of your life. You consciously create a "new" self that interacts with your companion in a new way. In addition, your "new" self interacts with the rest of the world with more Compassion and less Anger.

Finish The Old Script

Be aware that you are involved in two separate activities:

• Writing a new script for the emerging personality.

• Finishing the last act of the old script with the "old" personality.

Take the time to finish the old script while writing the new one. This provides a balance of past, present, and future activity. In your excitement over the new script, the old script is easily forgotten. Ignoring the old script while you try to read from the new one creates confusion rather than clarity.

Finishing the last act of the old script allows you the opportunity to squeeze all available knowledge from it. This means that you will be even better at the new one. Question it to determine the positive **and** negative learning that it brought. Understand the full spectrum of every experience. Move through any illusion that labels the old script "bad." Be thankful, for past experiences prepare you for new growth.

Complete the final act of the old script with a feeling of inner satisfaction for the path that you have walked. Develop an appreciation for the person that you are becoming and for the process that takes you there.

Respect The Process

This process of balance is extremely delicate. Everything progresses slowly and methodically. If any sub-personality weakens too fast, the other sub-personalities go crazy. They struggle to regain balance. Suddenly pulling the strength out of one sub-personality throws the whole system out of balance.

Compare your personal situation to a business that suddenly loses an employee. If the vice-president of daily operations suddenly loses his/her job, all the other employees must scramble to keep the business running smoothly. Without a person in this vital role, the business is in danger of collapse. Because a part of the whole is suddenly gone, the other employees are thrown into a state of confusion as they try to compensate for the loss.

Respect for the process of balance develops patience. You become aware of all the steps that take you from Point A to Point B. You automatically slow down in order to accurately label necessary steps. Objective observation and evaluation take a little extra time. Small adjustments here and there provide for a smooth transition period.

Find the primary lesson that each experience contains. Then look a little deeper to find the myriad of other lessons that is often intertwined. Recognize that each lesson, no matter how subtle, provides balance for a sub-personality somewhere within. By identifying which sub-personality is affected, you have greater understanding and appreciation for the process of balance. Understanding the intricacies of the process becomes a fascinating part of your journey. This understanding allows you increased participation in the conscious co-creation of your emerging personality.

TAKING THE CHALLENGE

*"Take the challenge to be proactive: to find, investigate, and explore
the challenging parts of Self that are out of balance."*

Life is full of unique experiences that explain who you are. Each experience defines your current capabilities, i.e., your strengths and weaknesses. Challenging situations blatantly show you exactly what you can and cannot do. They specifically identify what you could have done or said; how you could have reacted; what you will do the next time. They often provide the greatest opportunities for self-observation and inner growth.

Challenging situations pull you up into your potential. Every time you stretch, you grow. **Trying** sets the process in motion. Each **try** gives you credit on the inner levels for movement. Each **try** tells your Oversoul that you are ready for growth.

Challenging situations push you deep into your inner resources. In order to survive emotionally and/or physically, you reach into places inside of yourself that you did not even know existed. You may be pushed beyond your ordinary limits. Once you do this, you know that you will never be the same. These situations change you forever. These changes may be enormous or they may be subtle. But because you stretch deeper into your depths, you grow in one way or another.

A Measurement Of Inner Growth

Challenging situations are wonderful measurements of inner growth. They provide the opportunity to objectively evaluate today's reactions compared to how you would have reacted three months ago, six months ago, or a year ago. Challenging situations teach you how to:

Remain centered.

Think clearly.

Observe and listen objectively.

Change.

Flow with experience.

Learn from experience.

It does not matter if you did not move through the situation "perfectly." It only matters that you recognize where you were, where you are, and where you are going.

Challenging Sub-Personalities

Challenging situations bring out challenging sub-personalities. These sub-personalities often stay buried in ordinary situations. They are always there, but lie beneath the surface. They are easy to ignore until someone or something pulls them to the surface. Challenging situations force you to deal with these sub-personalities.

Most people wait for challenging situations before they address these sub-personalities. As long as life is relatively smooth, it is easy to ignore these aspects of Self. They lay dormant, quietly waiting for the right situation to pull them into action.

Proactive Vs. Reactive Learning

When you wait for challenging situations to pull these sub-personalities to the surface, your learning is "reactive." ***Reactive learning is passive learning.*** This means that if you sit around long enough, something will happen to ***make*** you learn. In the previous chapter, a friend's betrayal forced the evaluation of his/her strengths and weaknesses, as well as the evaluation of Self.

The opposite of reactive learning is "proactive" learning. Proactive learning means—

actively searching for growth;

being prepared for any challenge that flows your way;

welcoming every opportunity as a chance to learn more about who and what you are;

challenging yourself to find weaknesses;

and,

actively releasing all that you no longer need.

Proactive learning is active learning. A proactive person objectively observes and evaluates the friendship ***now.*** Without judgment or criticism, a proactive person understands the friend's current capabilities. Recognition of his/her need to gossip allows you to stop and think before you speak.

Sooner or later, you will evaluate the friendship. This can be done now (proactive), or later (reactive). You may want a friend with certain characteristics so much that you endow him/her with characteristics that he/she does not possess. Then, when he/she does not live up to your expectations, you are crushed. Recognize your friend's limitations before you are hurt. Avoid an unpleasant situation by objectively observing, listening, and evaluating.

Proactive Choices

Your goals for this lifeline are predetermined in the contract that you create with your Oversoul before you are born. Choose how to achieve these goals in the shortest, easiest, most pleasant (least objectionable) way. Cultivate patience. Stop, think, wait, and evaluate your options. Examine each one from implementation to completion. Ask yourself the following questions:

What obstacles might be in my way?

How will I move through them?

Is there another way that might be smoother?

If I choose a bumpy route, am I prepared for the bumps?

Feel the energy that is behind your course of action:

Is it smooth or bumpy?

Does it flow with my choice, or in another direction?

If it flows in another direction, does it lead to a better plan?

Feel the results of your choice:

Are the results ones that I can live with?

Ask your Oversoul to show you any obstacles that you overlooked, as well as alternative avenues of action. Once you make a choice, ask your Oversoul to communicate with everyone and everything involved in the process. Ask that everything be prepared on the inner levels first, similar to a dress rehearsal. Then, when you actually go through the process, everything is more likely to flow smoothly. Being proactive means moving from Point A to Point B in the least complicated, most efficient way possible.

Take The Challenge

Challenging situations and the sub-personalities that they evoke are always opportunities. A woodworker starts with a unique piece of wood. He recognizes the capabilities and potential of each piece. Knotholes are weaknesses. Yet with a little creativity, the uniqueness of a knothole adds to the beauty of a finished piece. A woodworker appreciates the knothole. He works with it, not against it.

Take the challenge to be proactive: to find, investigate, and explore the challenging parts of Self that are out of balance. Denial or avoidance, consciously or unconsciously, keeps doors closed. Closed doors mean no movement, no growth. Confronting these parts of Self opens doors that are tightly locked. Opening these doors presents choices and options—as well as a deeper understanding of Self, Oversoul, and God-Mind.

173

IDENTIFYING THE PLAYERS

*"You cannot ignore one of the players, or that
player will run rampant."*

Awareness of sub-personalities gives you a greater working knowledge of Self. Understanding that many players contribute to the whole allows you to now take command of your team. To be an effective captain, you must be able to correctly identify all the players.

Because your sub-personalities are all so interconnected, it is important that each one be properly identified. You may identify one sub-personality and think your job is done. But upon further examination you may find that one sub-personality is actually several sub-personalities intertwined.

For example, you may identify Love as one of your sub-personalities. However, Love often recruits several sub-personalities to play on its team. Fear, Guilt, Anger, Jealously, Control, Manipulation, Possessiveness, and Suffocation are a few of the sub-personalities that often team up with Love. When you want to express Love, you send Love to the front lines. But if you do not recognize that other sub-personalities are also moving to the front, you may be surprised at the response to your message.

You know that whatever you send out returns one way or another. When you send out only Love, only Love can come back. When something other than Love returns to you, understand that this is a clue that you have not accurately identified all of the players. The sub-personalities that you **think** you send out may be quite different from what actually goes out.

Happiness may be intertwined with Jealousy. When you are happy for someone, you send out the sub-personality named Happiness. But maybe Jealousy thinks **you** should be the recipient of good fortune, so it tags along.

You may have an obligation to fulfill, so you send out Sharing. However, Play wants to go sailing, so it teams up with Resentment. Together they try to overpower Sharing. Then Sharing talks Guilt into helping it move forward into fulfilling the obligation. No wonder sometimes you feel like you are pulled in ten different directions at once—often you are!

Gain Control

On some level of awareness, you always know what is happening. The difference is that now you bring that awareness forward into your conscious mind. Previously, your **team members** controlled **you.** Now you reverse the role so that **you** control the **team members.**

Sometimes when you deny these negative sub-personalities you somehow feel absolved of the responsibility of their actions. Rather than utilize your negative sub-personalities consciously, you simply deny their existence. Since you abdicate your role as leader, they constantly fight for control.

Society itself implies that negative is "bad" and "wrong." Negative is not "bad" or "wrong." Negative is just negative. **Negative sub-personalities are not "bad" or "wrong." They are important to the overall inner balance of Self.** Without judgment or criticism, simply acknowledge what does or does not exist. Then determine if any sub-personality is stronger than necessary. If so, release all that you no longer need up to your Oversoul.

Your Spiritual Journey

Sometimes people think that acknowledgment of negative sub-personalities means they also have to accept society's implications that **they** are "bad" or "wrong." They think that it is not possible to be a spiritual person if negative sub-personalities exist within. After all, how can you justify inner spirituality if you contain Fear, Guilt, Anger, Jealousy, Control, Manipulation, Possessiveness, or Suffocation?

You are a microcosm of the macrocosm. Whatever is within you, is also within God-Mind. **God-Mind is neither positive nor negative, but contains both. Positive and negative are both expressions of God-Mind. You are here to experience both.** How can you share your understanding of the negative with God-Mind if you refuse to acknowledge its existence within? If you ignore the negative within, then how can you explain:

What negative feels like?

How it affects physical, mental, and spiritual health?

How it affects quality of life?

To understand the microcosm (you) as well as the macrocosm (God-Mind), the negative must be explored and understood. The negative is part of the totality of All That Is. Negative is a part of you, and is rich with knowledge.

Calling yourself a "spiritual person" is easy when you only acknowledge the positive within. You may find this a more difficult label to accept when you acknowledge the negatives. Now you start vacillating. You send a mixed message to yourself that says, "I am a spiritual person as long as I am not Fearful, Guilty, Angry, Jealous, Controlling,

Manipulating, Possessive, Suffocating, etc." This translates into, "Sometimes I am okay and sometimes I am not." Recognition that positive and negative are both expressions of God-Mind creates the realization that you are acceptable as is.

Positive Sub-Personalities

Society implies that positive sub-personalities such as Happiness, Calm, Peace, Joy, Love, and Patience are the only acceptable ones to express. These are all very fine sub-personalities. However, if your negative sub-personalities were fed more than your positive ones, they are naturally stronger. Positive ones must literally fight to hold their space.

If Unhappiness is strong, it will do its best to keep Happiness weak; a strong Tension will keep Calm weak; Turbulence tries to keep Peace under control. This fighting keeps you from fully experiencing the expression of the positive aspects of Self.

Acknowledge All Sub-Personalities

Acknowledging positive sub-personalities is wonderful. Acknowledging negative sub-personalities is equally as wonderful. Learning intensifies as you explore the full spectrum of who you actually are.

When you first acknowledge these negative sub-personalities you may feel guilty for containing such "bad" qualities. Feeling guilty is often part of the process. You have old habit responses that say you "should not" contain anything negative. Understand that negative sub-personalities are important aspects of inner balance.

Whatever you find within, identify it immediately. Once identified, it is acknowledged. Once acknowledged, it can be accepted as part of the whole. Then it can be objectively evaluated to find out how strong or weak it is. You can make effective decisions concerning its future role.

Release Illusions

Release the illusion that "you should only contain positive sub-personalities." Negative sub-personalities contain many pieces of your personal puzzle. Be thankful for challenging situations and people that pull these negative sub-personalities to the front lines. They help you acknowledge aspects of Self that you might otherwise deny and/or avoid.

Ask your Oversoul to help you recognize the sub-personalities that are too strong for the part that you now play. Release the extra energy that comprises them up to your Oversoul. Ask to be shown the ones that are weak and in need of strength. Ask your Oversoul for the experiences and energy that will strengthen these aspects of Self.

Are You Ready?

Even though identifying the players may at times prove painful, even humbling, it is a necessary part of the process. Any qualified leader knows the strengths and weaknesses of every participant. This is the only way that a team can effectively function as a unit.

You cannot ignore one of the players or that player will run rampant. In the same way, you cannot lump two, three, or more players together and call them one player. Each player has its own individuality that contributes to the whole. And every team needs one leader. Are you ready and willing to accurately identify your players and take command of your team?

RECYCLING YOUR ENERGY

"Consciously develop a habit response that allows you to recycle the energy of every experience as it occurs."

When it is time for you to have a particular experience, your Oversoul sends the necessary energy into the outer world. This energy has shape, weight, color, and consistency, forming a colorful living pattern. On some level of awareness, you see this pattern and follow it. This pattern may lead to people, places, or things. As you use the energy, the energy transfers itself from the outer world into your auric field. When the energy transfer is complete, the experience is over.

Once in your aura, the energy of that experience is consumed by your sub-personalities. The experience determines which sub-personality gets the energy. If the experience was stressful, the energy feeds Stress; if the experience was peaceful, the energy feeds Peace, etc.

The color of this energy always matches the color of the sub-personality that gets fed. In other words, the energy that "funds" stressful experiences is the same color as the sub-personality Stress. Stress within your aura grows stronger with each stressful experience unless you know how to move this stress-containing energy back to its source—your Oversoul.

Once aware of the process, you can make conscious choices. You can choose to keep the stress energy or give it back to your Oversoul. Keeping it feeds Stress. Giving the energy back to your Oversoul releases the accumulated feelings of stress experiences from your aura. You retain the knowledge of your experiences without keeping the energy that brought the knowledge to you.

This process creates a cycle. Your Oversoul sends the energy for an experience into the outer world. You transfer the energy into your auric field as you move through the experience. Then you return the energy to your Oversoul once the experience is complete. This allows your Oversoul to clean, re-color, and re-cast the energy in another direction. The ultimate recycling program!

Conscious Decisions

Every time you make a conscious decision to return this energy to your Oversoul, **you** maintain your power. You stop strengthening sub-personalities that are already strong enough. Sub-personalities are fed in this manner for lifelines. They grow stronger and stronger as their particular energy accumulates.

When that role is over and that personality no longer necessary, then it is time to release the energy that created that specific personality. There are three primary ways that your Oversoul does this:

- Accidents

- Illness

- Between lifelines

Accidents and illness are the most common. For instance, many people have personality changes as a result of accidents and illness. The severity of these incidences determines how dramatically the personality changes. These occurrences create cellular changes in the physical structure as well as in the aura. These changes occur when your Oversoul recalls some of the no-longer-necessary energy. Your Oversoul also retrieves some of this energy between lifelines.

Once you become aware of this process, you become a conscious co-creator of Self. Together with your Oversoul you can create a new personality by consciously directing this energy as it comes into your aura. You can allow it to stay, knowing which sub-personality it will make stronger. Or you can choose to direct it up to your Oversoul.

You Are A Recipe

Your personality is like a recipe. You have a cupful of this sub-personality, a tablespoon of that one, and a dash of another. This blend forms the total personality you choose to express in this lifeline.

When you choose to change your personality, you are like the proverbial horse rider who decides to change horses in the middle of the stream. In the middle of this lifeline, you choose to take on an entirely different role. People used to have to wait for physical death and another lifeline to do this. With physical death, people release to their Oversoul all that they no longer need. Then, the next lifeline is chosen. Rather than waiting for physical death, you can release what you do not need now. You can consciously choose your next role and the personality traits that you need to support that role. This is a momentous step forward in self-awareness.

Know Your Ingredients

The more you know about the ingredients of your sub-personalities, the greater the ability you have to consciously co-create with your Oversoul. Develop an awareness of the energy color that feeds each sub-personality. Then, while you are in the process of re-creating your personality, you can more easily identify what you need or want to keep.

Energy colors vary from one individual to the next. Each person is unique, which means each person has his/her own unique blend of colors. The same color within one aura may mean something entirely different within another. Use the interpretations in the following chapters as guidelines, remembering that colors vary from person to person. Ask your Oversoul to explain how particular colors relate to you.

Your Colors Affect Your World

You look at the outer world through the colors of the energy that surround you. If your aura is full of red energy, the world has a red tint to it. If your aura is full of orange energy, the world has an orange tint. Whether your aura is dark and muddied or clean and clear, your world is colored by the colors of your aura contents. The colors surrounding you color your world.

Releasing excess colored energy from your aura to your Oversoul allows you to see the world through a clearer, cleaner aura. You see the world as it is rather than through the colors of your own experiences.

Feeding Sub-Personalities

Sub-personalities grow in proportion to the amount of colored energy that they are fed. Red energy feeds red sub-personalities, orange energy feeds orange sub-personalities, etc.

When these sub-personalities are fed well, it may become difficult to distinguish between them and the real you. The stronger they become, the more eager they are to take over. They very patiently wait for the right opportunity. Compare them to your taste buds. Your taste buds will rule you if you let them. Long after your physical body is full, your taste buds often tell you to continue eating. When they are in control, they also direct you to put unhealthy foods into your body.

In the same way, sub-personalities will rule the real you whenever possible. You actually battle with these sub-personalities over who will rule your life at any given moment. Sometimes this battle wears you out. You give up and your sub-personalities battle amongst themselves. When you lose control over them, the ones that were fed the most are the winners.

Work From Your Center

Because sub-personalities are strengthened by energy from your Oversoul, you can weaken them by reversing the process. Standing in your center, you take back your control over these sub-personalities. The chapter *Into The Silence*, **Section I** details how to build your center. You literally build a place that anchors you in the strength of your Oversoul and God-Mind.

If you step out of your center, whichever sub-personality is the most powerful at the moment may take control over **you**. If this happens, simply start the breathing technique from that chapter. Acting as a vacuum, your breath pulls you back into your center. From your center, start over.

Use the mind as a tool. **Will** the excess energy up to your Oversoul. You **will** your arms and legs to move all the time—and they move. In the same way, **will** the excess color of the sub-personality up to your Oversoul. Watch it move out of your aura and up the channel that connects you to your Oversoul. Know that something actually happens. This goes beyond visualization. You are in the process of weakening a too-strong sub-personality to bring Self into balance.

Continue to will the energy up to your Oversoul. Tell your Oversoul to take all that you no longer need, returning only enough to maintain inner balance. You cannot suddenly lose a part of Self or the whole will be thrown into chaos. This explains why you sometimes feel like you take one step forward and two steps back. There are many, many aspects of Self striving to maintain inner balance.

When you walk along a narrow ledge and start to lose your balance, what happens? You sway to the left, then to the right, and your arms flail about. This continues until you either regain your balance, or you fall off and start over again. This also happens on the inner levels. When you take that step forward, you are unaware of how much of Self is thrown off balance. Sometimes, you have to take a couple of steps backward on the inner levels to get everything adjusted to the new direction. Sometimes, you have to stop and start over.

Illusion may try to make you feel tremendously discouraged. Reality explains that you actually accomplish a great deal on the inner levels and that victory is in progress.

Clearing Your Minds

As the excess energy moves out of your aura and body, the conscious mind becomes clearer and cleaner. As the conscious mind empties out, information from childhood, perhaps even other lifelines, starts moving forward from the subconscious mind. In turn, the subconscious mind becomes clearer and cleaner, allowing information from the superconscious mind to move forward through the subconscious and into the conscious mind.

Step by step, the process takes place. Step by step, the doorways to the next levels of learning open. All you have to do is be a clean receiver, paying attention to the information and knowledge that trickles forward into your conscious mind. There is nothing mysterious or difficult about the process. Anyone can do it. As with most worthwhile activities, you need patience and perseverance.

As the past is released layer by layer, awareness of what already exists expands. You begin to understand who you are, as well as the experiences that brought you to this point. By remaining centered and calm you maintain your focus as an objective observer. Releasing excess energy allows the color of your world to change. You see it as it is, rather than through the colors of your own experiences.

All that you no longer need drops away. New challenges and changes move into the picture. Weaknesses are strengthened, strengths become stronger. You move swiftly and steadily into the next phase of your life. You become increasingly centered and calm because *you* control the sub-personalities. With this new internal order there is less confusion to pull your attention outward. Growth accelerates because you extract more conscious knowledge from each experience.

With this new control, you continue to   your center. You feel the depth of the connection between Self, Oversoul, and God-Mind. Vertical movement is easier because you do not have to battle powerful sub-personalities that pull your attention horizontally.

"Predicting" The Future

With awareness of this energy, you can even "predict" the future. You can look (or feel) to see if energy exists to "fund" a particular experience. An event occurs only when an energy pattern exists for it to occur. In essence, you do not "predict" anything. You are only aware of what already exists. Just because something is not yet manifest in this reality does not mean that it does not exist. You do not become "psychic," you merely fine-tune your awareness of what is.

Consciously Recycle Your Energy

Consciously develop a habit response that allows you to recycle the energy of every experience as it occurs. Recycling the energy of your experiences accelerates your learning process, quickly moving new and different experiences into your life. In addition, this clearing and cleansing process reveals more of who and what you are, and continues to specifically define your potential. Consciously recycling your energy is another fascinating step on the journey of self-awareness.

EXPLORING THE REDS

*"Whenever you speak in red, you provide the ammunition
for the other person to speak in red."*

When your Oversoul sends red energy into the outer world, most likely your experience will be creative, sexual, angry, bitter, resentful, and/or hateful. Moving through the experience, you transfer the red energy from the outer world into your aura. This energy feeds the sub-personality that matches that particular shade of red.

The red energy is always neutral—it is your reaction that labels it "positive" or "negative." You can, for instance, create by building or destroying. Sexual experiences can be wonderful or degrading. Likewise, anger, bitterness, resentment, and hate are all neutral. They also have both positive and negative aspects.

Once you understand that all sub-personalities are an important part of your personal recipe, you can objectively evaluate them to determine their strengths and weaknesses. This allows you to understand both positive and negative aspects of each sub-personality. In addition, you recognize that the sub-personality is neutral. This new perspective gives you back your power. In this way, you learn to use your sub-personalities without them using you. Any time that they are **not** in a neutral position means that they are out of balance. As captain of your team, it is your responsibility to consciously bring them into balance.

Sometimes it is easy to recognize when sub-personalities are out of balance. Anger is an excellent example with which most people can identify. There are times when there is no doubt in your mind that Anger controls you. You feel the strength of Inner Anger. You know that Anger is very much out of balance. Anger was fed with so much red energy that you can feel that it really does have a mind of its own. **You** are no longer in control. Instead, Anger controls **you**. You may feel helpless once it is in action.

Sometimes it is not so easy to recognize when sub-personalities are out of balance. Anger also has its subtle side. Consider the following questions:

Do you get angry when—

You drop something and it breaks?

You stub your toe?

Other drivers are in your way?

The paper is late?

The news reports something you consider "bad?"

The weather takes a turn for the worse?

You lose something?

If you answered "yes" to any of the above questions, your Anger is out of balance. These are all subtle feelings of anger. When Anger is in balance none of the above ever evokes an anger response. You may **think** that Anger is in balance, but when you pay attention to all the little subtleties, you may find that it is not. Often people who deny that Anger exists within are full of Anger. They simply suppress the emotion, therefore denying its existence.

Bitterness, Resentment, and Hate often take on the same subtle tones as Anger. The sub-personalities like to stay hidden so that you are unable to find and label them. Once labeled, you have something to work with. This means that you can consciously drain them of their power. Staying hidden allows them to keep their power.

When sub-personalities are out of balance, they weaken who and what you are. They become toxic to you and your physical body. Even allowing these sub-personalities to be out of balance for "good" reasons creates toxins. You may feel Anger toward the "injustices" in the world; Bitterness toward a person who treated you unfairly; Resentment toward a life that does not meet your expectations. These are all legitimate feelings with legitimate reasons for existing. Yet, these feelings all create in a negative way. They create mental, emotional, physical, and spiritual ill-health.

As sub-personalities grow stronger, their consciousness becomes more complex. They begin creating within your aura. Anger, Bitterness, Resentment, and Hate create the additional sub-personalities of Unforgiveness, Irritability, and Frustration. Now, you are not the only one who creates within your space. The sub-personalities also have the power to create. These sub-personalities will continue to create if you do not take your power back.

Take Your Power Back

Claim your role as captain of your team. Take your power back. Breathe yourself into your center. With your mind, will the excess red energy out of these sub-personalities. Pull it in from your aura, into your center, and up the channel to your Oversoul. With your mind, drain the sub-personality of its excess strength whenever you think about it— during meditation, or simply as you do your daily tasks.

Ask your Oversoul to explain all the lessons that your strong sub-personality taught you. Understand it thoroughly—all the positives and negatives. You will **know** when the draining is complete. Experiences that once would evoke a response of Anger, Bitterness, Resentment, or Hate no longer do so. The sub-personality that would have reacted is now closer to balance. You can use it when necessary, but it can no longer use you.

Positive Aspects

As you release this excess energy, it passes before your inner eye on the way up to your Oversoul. As it does, this is an opportunity to understand this member of your personality. You may be familiar with the negative aspects of Anger, Bitterness, Resentment, and Hate. But for these sub-personalities to come into balance, you must also understand their positive aspects. All sub-personalities have a reason for existing. All sub-personalities are neutral. For you to **know** this, you must **know** the positive aspects of all parts of Self.

To begin the process, consider some of the positive aspects of these sub-personalities:

Motivation. Anger, Bitterness, Resentment, and Hate build energy within. When these emotions become intense, they motivate you to get up, get going, and do something! This may be something as simple as cleaning and organizing your physical space, such as home or office. Or, it may be the motivation that you need for a major life change.

Courage. When you are angry, bitter, resentful, and/or hateful enough, you finally get the courage to stand up for yourself. Finally, you are able to say, "I am worth fighting for!"

Focus. The strength of these sub-personalities causes you to focus all your attention in one place. When Hate has control, you focus on Hate and Hate alone. Regardless of what happens in the outer world, you remain focused on the subject before you. That ability to focus can be applied in any area of your life—from driving a car to meditation.

Clarification. Buried feelings often pop out in the middle of heated discussions. Without even thinking, what you really feel sometimes jumps out of your mouth. These emotions push you so deep so fast that you suddenly have no choice but to acknowledge how you really feel.

Control. These emotions emanate from your being. When you want others at a distance for whatever reason, these sub-personalities send a clear signal to stay out of your space. They help you keep control of any given situation. Even when you feel vulnerable and/or threatened, these sub-personalities can effectively cover fear and insecurity.

Power. These sub-personalities may frighten people. Out of fear, others may voluntarily give their power to you. It is your choice whether you keep or return that power.

More of the same. The outer world reflects your Anger, Bitterness, Resentment, and Hate back to you. This allows you to study your inner state of being by observing the outer. Without getting too close to Self, you see what you really look like in a safe way.

As a microcosm of the macrocosm, you contain a part of All That Is. While you are not Anger, Bitterness, Resentment, and Hate in and of themselves, you contain some of each simply because they exist.

Clean Up Your Words

When these sub-personalities become strong and out-of-balance, they create inner pain and discomfort. When this occurs, you want to remove these feelings. The most common way to **try** to remove them is to **try** to give them to others. People do this subtly and/or overtly with hurting remarks or sharp retorts. Sometimes people **try** to remove these feelings by inflicting physical or emotional pain on themselves. Neither **excuses** the actions, only **explains** the actions.

When you speak in Anger, Bitterness, Resentment, and Hate, you speak in red. This releases some of the sub-personality's strength. However, this red energy then feeds the same sub-personality of others. For example, when the red of bitterness comes out of your mouth, it moves into the other person's aura. If this person has a strong sub-personality named Bitterness, Bitterness latches onto that energy. With this additional strength, the other person can continue to hurl Bitterness back at you.

For this reason, send your message without sending the red energy along with it. At the same time, do not deny or ignore your own feelings. When you feel Bitterness rise up, acknowledge it. Then pass the red energy of Bitterness up to your Oversoul.

Do not keep this red energy and play with it. Do not send it out your mouth. Do not feed your own or anyone else's sub-personality. Will this energy out of Self. Tell your Oversoul to pass your feelings of Bitterness on to the other person via his/her Oversoul. That person will receive those feelings of Bitterness at the discretion of his/her Oversoul. The involved Oversouls determine the fate of the Bitterness energy, not you. When you do speak, your words are clear. They are not colored with red.

By doing this, you actually perform two tasks at once:

1. Release the colored energy of your emotions up to your Oversoul.

2. Speak clear words out of your mouth.

Whenever you speak in red, you provide the ammunition for the other person to speak back to you in red. You feed their sub-personalities. You complete a cycle that circulates back and forth between you. Red energy going out means red energy coming back. Break the cycle. Retain your power instead of giving it away.

Any time these feelings rise within, express them through the involved Oversouls. Utilize the inner levels to yell, scream, cry, and swear at the other person. This is a much cleaner way of handling the situation. Without dumping into your environment or into any part of Self, your Oversoul cleans you up as you go. This allows acknowledgment and full expression of emotions without judgment or criticism of Self. In awareness, you simply acknowledge what is. In addition, you do not give extra strength to sub-personalities that are already strong enough.

Anchor Yourself

Before you allow these emotions to come out, take a moment to breathe yourself into your center. As long as you remain in your center, anchored in the strength of your Oversoul and God-Mind, you are safe. Take time to anchor yourself. You are separate from these emotions. They are a part of you, but they are not you. **You** control **them**.

Because these emotions already exist within, no one or no situation makes you react. These situations only draw out what already exists. Drain the strength from these sub-personalities without waiting for a person or situation to do it for you. Be proactive.

Observe your reactions of today. Compare them to your reactions of three months ago and even to last year. Acknowledge where you were and where you are now. The change may seem slow, but this is the way that balanced change occurs.

Keep Your Power

Keep in mind that even though your sub-personalities come into balance, they can at any time become unbalanced. Whenever you keep the energy of any experience, sub-personalities grow. They can also grow from the horizontal flow of psychic energy sent by other people. Any time this happens, ask your Oversoul to send this energy back to its rightful owner. Know your sub-personalities well enough to recognize when and how they start to become unbalanced. Notice the instant they become too strong. Keep your power.

Nurture Weak Sub-Personalities

As your strong sub-personalities come into balance, nurture your weak ones. Ask your Oversoul to send pink energy into Love, Compassion, Joy, Softness, and Gentleness. Watch your being as it is flooded with clear, clean colors. Feel the difference that this makes in your aura and deep within Self. Bring clear, clean colors into all areas of your life. Decide with care which inner colors you wish your outer world to reflect back to you.

In order for any of your positive sub-personalities to grow, send back to your Oversoul the colors that create them. When you feel creative, thank your Oversoul for sending creative red energy. When the experience is over, send the red energy back. Your Oversoul then recycles it into a new, better experience. Every time you give something back to your Oversoul, an opportunity for growth results.

As sub-personalities change, the cellular structure of your physical body automatically changes. The sub-personalities that were too strong and created your body in a negative way are in balance. The ones that were weak are now nurtured to re-create your body in a positive way.

While you may think of your body as solid, it is not. It is simply a collection of matter that builds itself around and through the sub-personalities. As the energy of the sub-personalities alters, the matter that comprises your body also alters. The entire cellular structure changes, becoming clearer and less dense, as balance progresses.

You feel and function better on all levels. And when you do start to get out of balance, you become uncomfortable very quickly. You are anxious to get the imbalance corrected, and you are grateful for the people and situations that point out your imbalances.

THE EGO OF ORANGE

*"When Ego and Self-Esteem are in balance, you can walk
into any situation knowing that you are okay 'as is.' "*

Ego is a sub-personality that gathers its strength from orange energy. As with all sub-personalities, Ego is neither positive nor negative, but neutral. Ego is an important ingredient in your personal recipe. Ego says that you can have or do anything you want. This means fulfilling any physical, emotional, mental, spiritual, and/or material want or wish.

When Self-Esteem whispers, "I can't do it; I don't know how; I'm not capable, " Ego takes control. Ego recognizes that Self-Esteem may never get going. Ego pushes right through these self-imposed limitations, moving you toward your goal.

Ego defines your capabilities, then pushes you into your potential, encouraging you to experiment with new and different avenues of action. Even when the odds appear insurmountable, Ego forces you to pursue your goals. Ego helps you acknowledge who you are and what you can do. Without Ego, there are times when you would never move at all. Ego is a necessary part of the whole.

A Key Player

Ego initiates movement. A key player among the other sub-personalities, its role is similar to that of a quarterback on a football team. A good quarterback knows the strengths and weaknesses of his team. He passes the ball to other players who in turn move the ball down the field toward the goal.

If the other players always throw the ball back to him, he soon realizes that winning the game is his responsibility. He then stops passing the ball to the other players, keeps it for himself, and does his best to get to the goal. If this continues, the other players become lazy and weak. On the other hand, the quarterback becomes strong and independent.

This is what happens to Ego. There is a goal. Energy comes in from your Oversoul to move you toward the goal. Ego evaluates the goal and determines that you can get there. Ego directs the other sub-personalities to move. They give the energy back to Ego. Ego says, "Somebody has to do this!" and off it goes.

This has happened so often that Ego does not even consult the other sub-personalities. It simply keeps the energy and does whatever is necessary to get you where it thinks you need to be. Throughout many lifelines Ego becomes strong and out-of-balance.

Self-Esteem

As soon as Ego recognizes a goal, it passes the ball to Self-Esteem. Weak from inactivity, Self-Esteem immediately starts moaning, "I can't do it; it's too hard," and passes the ball back. When this repeatedly happens, Ego stops passing the ball to Self-Esteem. Why should it? It knows what will happen. Self-Esteem grows weaker while Ego grows stronger. Ego really has no choice.

This happens so often that you forget that Ego and Self-Esteem are separate. No longer able to separate them, you think that they are the same. The reality is that a powerful Ego most often means a weak Self-Esteem.

Psychic Energy Feeds Ego

Your psychic energy is your personal energy. This horizontal flow of energy is orange. Whenever you talk, this energy moves your words out of your mouth. Regardless of the color of your words, the flow that carries it is orange. When you speak by directing the flow of this energy vertically, you send it to your Oversoul for recycling. When you allow the energy to flow horizontally, it is up for grabs. Even though it is a part of you, other people can use it. You willingly give it. They willingly take it.

The orange psychic energy that you expend floats into others' auras. When their Egos are out of balance, they grab at the chance for the additional energy. This energy gives their Egos additional strength.

When your Ego is out of balance, it also takes the psychic energy of others and incorporates it into itself. In this way, you literally allow a part of others to live within a member of your personality.

When others tell you how wonderful and great you are (for whatever reasons), this is orange Ego energy flowing toward your Ego sub-personality. Once you allow that orange Ego energy into your aura, your Ego gobbles up that energy. You eventually lose your identity because you are full of others' orange Ego energy.

You forget who you are, and become what the energy says you are. **You** become lost because your Ego is no longer just **your** sub-personality, rather it is the combination of Ego sub-personalities of many, many people which now lives within your aura.

External Feedback

Any external feedback that others send to you feeds Ego. Only by giving it back via the involved Oversouls, can Ego find balance. Ego has grown for many lifelines, gaining its identity from many different sources. Bringing it into balance must be done slowly to help the other sub-personalities adjust to the change.

The weak sub-personalities must become strong and learn to function all over again. Suddenly removing all of Ego's excess energy would place a chaotic burden on them. For this reason, deflate the strength of Ego slowly.

Ego Out Of Balance

With an Ego that is too strong, Self-Esteem becomes unable to say, "I am okay as is." You now **need** others to do this for you. This distorts your reality. Ego thinks it is extremely important. Ego thinks that it is the center of the universe. Then, it does its best to convince you of the same. This further increases its power.

Ego tells you that everyone watches and listens to you wherever you go, whatever you do. Because who you are is buried, you believe it. You express this every day in very simple ways.

You accidentally hit the horn in traffic—you feel foolish, silently melting into your seat. Yet, who else really cares that your horn went off?

You get caught in unexpected wind and your hair becomes totally unmanageable. All day long, do you really think everyone in the office is laughing and talking about your hair? Who really cares besides you?

Your daughter wears a trendy outfit to go shopping with you. If she wears it, what will people think? An argument ensues while you try to force her to wear something else. Why do you care what they think?

At the last minute you notice a spot on your shirt. You do not have time to change. You feel uncomfortable because you think that everyone will see it. So what if they do? Do you think they will make it the prime topic of conversation for the evening?

You stumble over a few words while giving a speech. You chastise yourself for days— yet who else in the audience remembers the incident as vividly and as long as you?

How many things do you choose not to do because "What would people think?" Possible reactions of total strangers dictate your actions because you think everyone watches and listens to you. Most people have plenty of their own challenges. Believe it or not, your life is not their primary concern. Yes, you are a part of the universe—but you are not the center.

Is It Ego Or Self-Esteem?

Because Self-Esteem allowed itself to become weak, you **need** an extra powerful Ego. Ego maintains its importance by allowing Self-Esteem to be weak. Once it recognizes the weakened state of Self-Esteem, it does its best to control Self-Esteem.

Thus, Self-Esteem can only **try**. Self-Esteem **tries** to show that you feel good about Self. It **tries** to give the appearance that it has strength.

Be aware that Self-Esteem may bluff you into thinking that it is strong. But Self-Esteem is different than Ego. Self-Esteem is only strong when who you are is dependent solely on internal feedback. That means that your identity comes from within. Friends, family, possessions, occupation, etc. could disappear and you would still value yourself as is. When Self-Esteem is strong, you do not need the outer world to validate your existence. All you need is feedback from Self, Oversoul, and God-Mind.

Internal Feedback

Self-Esteem is fed from the orange psychic energy of your own internal "self-talk." Self-Esteem grows strong when fed positive internal self-talk, weak when fed negative internal self-talk.

When you consciously feed Self-Esteem positive internal self-talk, it grows stronger. This throws the partnership with powerful Ego out of balance. To correct this imbalance, ask your Oversoul to take all of the energy that Ego no longer needs. With your mind, will the bright orange energy of Ego up to your Oversoul. Thank Ego for all the extra work that it has done. Explain that Self-Esteem has grown. Both sub-personalities must adjust to the new balance.

As Self-Esteem gathers strength, you become less dependent on external feedback. Feelings of self-worth come from within instead of without. Requiring less external feedback puts life in perspective. With less power, Ego can no longer fool you into believing that you are the center of the universe.

This enhances your objective perspective on Self. Your actions become dependent on, "What do **I** think?" rather than "What do **others** think?" Internal feelings determine your actions. You recognize that no one really pays that much attention to you. You are not the center of the universe. You are merely an observer who is in the process of learning about Self, your Oversoul, and God-Mind. This is your ultimate purpose on Earth.

When you leave this reality, you do not take the knowledge or wisdom that you gave to others. You only take your own learning. The more you observe and listen to your world, the more you learn about Self, your Oversoul, and God-Mind; i.e., the more you have to take onto your next journey.

Balancing Ego

The energy of external feedback that lives within your aura keeps you from dialoguing with Self. Releasing this to your Oversoul gives you back the opportunity to communicate with the real you. Within your aura the sub-personality called Ego is clogged with the orange psychic "self-talk" energy of others.

As this moves out of your aura, direct your attention to Self-Esteem. Understand that it is weak and in need of extra care. When Self-Esteem declares "I'm not good enough, smart enough, pretty/handsome enough, etc.," take the time to **hear** these declarations. Do not deny or ignore them. Send those statements up to your Oversoul.

Replace them with affirmations of, "I am good enough, smart enough, pretty/handsome enough, etc." Affirmations consciously direct psychic energy into weak members of your personality. Send this positive internal self-talk up to your Oversoul also. Ask your Oversoul to send back only what Self-Esteem can handle. Just as Ego must be weakened in a balanced way, Self-Esteem must be strengthened in a balanced way.

The Process Of Balance

As these sub-personalities come into balance, recognize that it would not be comfortable for you to suddenly be without the external feedback. You may be an excellent cook. You appreciate the compliments that other people give you (external feedback), but you do not require them to appreciate your own skills. You already know that you are an excellent cook (internal feedback).

If you decide to learn a new skill, such as piloting a small plane, you may need the flight instructor's external feedback. When you have difficulty assessing your own strengths, external feedback is important. Sometimes you need others to validate current capabilities and potential.

External feedback provides opportunities to evaluate what exists within. A compliment from your flight instructor may not mean that you are ready for a solo flight. In the same way, compliments on your cooking talents probably do not mean that you are the greatest chef in the world. Acknowledge compliments. Allow them to validate what you already know. Then release this energy up to your Oversoul.

Ego is fed by keeping the energy of these compliments. The energy from compliments will also define you into something that you are not. The more power you give to Ego, the more control it takes. It will gladly fulfill any illusion that you wish—even dangerous ones such as a solo flight for which you may not be ready.

Negative external feedback also provides opportunities for self-evaluation. When Ego is out of balance it may tell you to disregard negative feedback. But sometimes this type of feedback is valuable. Sometimes people need to hear how others perceive them. Others always reflect a part of Self. Therefore it is important to listen to their words, to find out if there is any truth in them. They may see something to which you need to pay attention.

Sometimes Ego chooses to give this negative feedback to Self-Esteem to help keep it weak. When Self-Esteem is lazy and weak, it accepts this type of energy. As long as it stays weak, Ego will do all the work. Self-Esteem can continue its lazy ways.

Ego And Self-Esteem In Balance

When Ego and Self-Esteem are in balance, you can walk into any situation knowing that you are okay as is. You feel good about yourself. You express this naturally through your walk, talk, actions, and attitudes. You do not have to **try**. Self-Esteem allows you to feel good about yourself without a particular reason. You value external feedback, but it is not essential. When in balance, Ego motivates you but it is Self-Esteem that says "I can do it!"

EGO IN CONTROL

*"Ego has been the downfall of many.
It is strong, powerful, and sneaky."*

Ego does what is necessary to maintain its power, including subdividing itself. In other words, the consciousness of your sub-personality creates other sub-personalities. To bring Ego into balance, the following sub-personalities must also be brought into balance.

Guilt

Guilt is one of the more blatant sub-personalities of Ego. Guilt performs two primary functions for Ego:

1. Importance;

   and,

2. Responsibility.

Both make you feel needed as described below.

Importance

Guilt gives you importance in a variety of ways. Say you have a friend who has a life full of challenges. You know that she feels better after talking to you even though you feel drained. Yet you feel you must continue these conversations. After all, who else does she have? You feel guilty when thoughts of abandoning her enter your mind. Even though she is a drain on your mental health, her need for you makes you feel important. Guilt controls your actions. Instead of letting Guilt control you, stop and evaluate:

Did you create her life?

Are you responsible for her?

Do you feel like a dumping ground?

Is she interested in helping herself?

Is it you who she needs, or would anyone willing to listen do?

Does she want to put her life in order or on some level does she enjoy the confusion and turmoil?

Answer these questions by sending them up to your Oversoul. Ask for direction. You may find that instead of helping, you are interfering. Her challenges may be her motivation for change. Lessening her burdens may take away her opportunity for growth. Releasing her may mean releasing your opportunity to feel important and needed. Guilt **tries** to make you hang on. But **you** have to take control. Allowing her to have her own life in turn allows you to have yours.

Think about this. You have two children and a spouse that constantly make demands upon your time and energy. The occasional times that you tell them "no" you feel guilty. Is it necessary to feel guilty because you are unable to give beyond your capabilities?

Being responsible for everyone in the household acknowledges your importance. It makes you feel needed. In this case Guilt holds Ego close to you. Letting go of some Ego means letting others be responsible for themselves. Creating balance within allows others to do the same. Everyone around you is a reflection of Self. Whenever you want change in the outer world, the inner world must change first. Instead of asking others to change, change Self first.

Responsible

Guilt makes you feel responsible even when you are not. Guilt does this by telling you that you "should" have done this or that. The real you knows that if you could have done "this or that" you would have.

You may say, "I shouldn't have yelled at him, but I did. Now I feel guilty." While it may be true that you are in the process of bringing Anger into balance, it is not in balance yet. Do the best that you can with your current capabilities. Then evaluate the situation so you can do better the next time. That is all. Release these thoughts and feelings to your Oversoul, along with your need for Guilt.

Guilt makes you feel responsible for people/situations for which you are not responsible. Look at the way charities use guilt when they solicit money. They show pictures of starving and/or diseased children and animals brutally treated. Without even bothering to investigate the legitimacy of these organizations, many people simply send money. Guilt says "send money," so you do. Before sending money, it is important to first ask your Oversoul if this is a place that needs your money.

Guilt allows you to feel pressured by others to be someone that you are not; to give more of yourself than you are capable of giving. When you choose your own path, you often feel guilty for denying what other people want you to do.

For example, career choices create guilt for some people. Mom and Dad think you would make a great engineer. Without ever asking you, this is a career they assume you will follow. They may not ever take the time to know what is in your heart. Telling them otherwise can be difficult. The guilt you feel for not pleasing your parents can be very heavy.

If you live close to your family, they may automatically assume that you will be available at any time to help family members, regardless of your plans. Being true to yourself means denying the needs of others. Breaking out of this pattern creates tremendous guilt. When others control you through guilt, who you are often gets lost in the process.

As much as you may want to do something else, it sometimes becomes easier to let others control you rather than stand up for Self. When pleasing others means denying the needs of Self, weigh what you can and cannot live with. You may decide that it is easier to deny your own needs rather than live with the guilt of displeasing others. The additional weight of Guilt that others place on you (and you allow) would be too much. Although this may cause Resentment, you may choose to carry Resentment rather than Guilt. Guilt grabs the opportunity to take control of the situation.

When you choose to deny your own needs, thus damaging Self, do so in awareness. Becoming aware of what you do and the consequences of your decisions are the first steps to balance. Only by becoming aware can you move forward with the process of balance.

Continue to strengthen Self-Esteem, explaining your changes to the people around you via the involved Oversouls. Remember, you cannot change them. You can only change Self. Nor is it your responsibility to change them. However, it is your responsibility to respect their choices. Release them to their Oversouls, letting them go on their way. Have Compassion for them. Realize that they try to control with Guilt because they are afraid.

Sometimes when you are true to Self, Guilt gets fed anyway. Not being able to save a drowning person might allow Guilt to live on forever. Yet, perhaps this was the time and way that person chose to go. If you were able to save him/her, you might have interfered in his/her life pattern.

These are difficult calls to make. Each one is uniquely personal. That is why it is so important to open your inner channels of communication. Let your Oversoul instruct your reality. Release the need for illusion to guide you.

Guilt helps you hold onto other people. In the same way that other people try to control you with Guilt, you do the same. Listen to your words. Watch your actions. Look for the many subtle ways that you try to control with Guilt:

"Do this for me or I'll be hurt."

"If you go, I'll worry."

"You haven't written in ages; are you okay?"

"You should have been there for me!"

"You were out playing when I needed you!"

These kinds of words feed Guilt in others. On some level of awareness you know this. Release the need to control others through Guilt. If you have to use Guilt to control, then it is time to let go.

Controlling with Guilt can be even subtler. Greeting cards are full of guilt:

"Across the miles..." "Wish you were here..." "Christmas is not the same without you..."

These kinds of greetings hold sadness. This sadness also feeds Guilt. The recipient feels guilty that he/she is far away from the sender. Guilt subtly weaves itself into many of life's facets.

Whenever anyone tries to control you with Guilt, use this as an opportunity to evaluate Self. Is there any sub-personality within that tries to control others with Guilt? If so, as you release the need to control others through Guilt, others release their need to control you through Guilt.

Evaluate Guilt

Whenever you feel Guilt, evaluate your feelings. Ask yourself the following questions:

Is it time to make a change?

Do I expect too much from myself?

Am I really responsible for this person/situation?

Is Guilt in my life to make me feel important?

Do I try to control others through guilt?

Learning to correctly identify Guilt allows you to release it.

Guilt Is Like Glue

Guilt makes you feel uncomfortable with your own actions. This orange-brown substance is rubbery and coats like glue. This uncomfortable feeling coupled with its sticky substance keeps your actions in your conscious mind. The glue of Guilt will not let memories be released up to your Oversoul.

When Anger takes control, Guilt helps you remember the outburst. When Anger takes control again, Guilt reminds you of the previous incident. Guilt is the glue between your conscious mind and Anger. Eventually, the weight of Guilt becomes so heavy that you will do anything to get rid of it.

This means you finally take a look at Anger. The only way you can get rid of the glue of Guilt is to release the extra strength of Anger. In this way, **Guilt motivates you to change.**

The extra weight of Guilt pulls on your conscious mind until you can no longer ignore it. The weight of Guilt becomes progressively heavier. You simply do not have the strength to carry the experience around any more. One way or the other, you have no choice but to change. Even though you may not be eager to change, change becomes easier than carrying all that weight.

Judgment And Criticism

Judgment and criticism are also sub-personalities of Ego. They too, are fed with orange energy. You may not think of yourself as a judgmental or critical person. However, there are many ways of making many little judgments that elevate Self while putting others down. For instance do you pat yourself on the back because you:

Eat healthier food than others?

Exercise more?

Have more material possessions?

Handle your emotions better?

Ever think, "*I* wouldn't do that!"?

Meditate more?

Think you have more "spiritual" qualities?

Sometimes when you get to high school, you are so far removed from elementary school that you forget how hard those students struggle. You develop an attitude that says, "I can do it, why can't you?" At one time you were in elementary school, too. Whether in elementary or high school, each person struggles. Understand that every person is on a path to self-awareness. Respect the place on the path that others are on, regardless of where that place might be in comparison to your own personal journey.

Objectively observe the lessons of these people. Ask your Oversoul and God-Mind to send them blessings for their efforts as well as any help that they might need. Touch into Compassion from time to time. Compassion helps keep Ego from gaining excess power.

You may have a tendency to judge others against what is right for you. You have been taught to think, "How would I feel if I were him/her?" That is a fine first step. But the second step goes beyond that. The second step asks the questions, "How does **he/she** feel? What does **he/she** need?" Ask your Oversoul these questions. If it is for you to know, you will get an answer.

All the popular talk shows are wonderful examples of how judgmental people can be. The guests share their personal stories while the audience judges if their behavior is acceptable or unacceptable. Judging others is an Ego enhancer.

Judging others says, "You are not as good as I am," i.e., "**I** am too good for that." For example, because you are fifty and think you would not marry someone twenty does not make you right and someone else wrong. Life carries a variety of lessons as well as a variety of ways of learning those lessons.

Releasing the need to judge and criticize Self provides the opportunity to objectively observe Self. Then changes can be made where changes are needed. Accepting Self as is allows you to accept others as they are. Do your best to objectively observe others with Compassion and Understanding.

Other Forms Of Ego

Ego comes in a variety of forms. Continue to develop self-awareness so that you can identify and label them. Once labeled, **you** can take control. Merely send all the excess orange energy up to your Oversoul.

Other forms of Ego include:

POWER. You are not here to have power over anything. You are here to work with and to appreciate the natural abilities of All That Is.

SELF-AGGRANDIZEMENT. You are not more important than anyone else. You cannot be the boss if you do not have any workers. Workers merely establish who is the boss and who is not.

SUPERIORITY. You are not better than anyone else. You may have skills that someone else does not have, but they may have skills that you do not have. Being different from others does not make you better; it simply makes you different.

EMBARRASSMENT. Embarrassment allows the outer world to totally define you for the moment. Praise may embarrass you as quickly as criticism. Accept the compliments. Evaluate the criticism. Do the best that you can with the tools, experiences, and knowledge that you have. Accept Self as is in any given moment.

DEFENSIVENESS. Ego blocks out the words of other people. Learn to listen. Others may be aware of parts of Self that you cannot yet see. Evaluate all words spoken to you to determine their validity. Allow others to teach you.

STUBBORNNESS. Stubbornness is a wall of Ego that will not let the real you through. Stubbornness is a defense mechanism that prevents you from admitting, "I'm wrong; you're right." Acknowledging that someone else is right acknowledges that you need to grow. That can sometimes be a painful admission.

CONTROL AND MANIPULATION. Gain control of your life only long enough to give that control to your Oversoul and God-Mind. With increased self-awareness, become a conscious co-creator of your life.

MEDDLING. Release the need to play God-Mind. You did not create the challenges of others. Thus, it is not your place to solve them. On some level of awareness others want the satisfaction of solving their own challenges. Ask permission through the involved Oversouls before offering help to anyone. Find out if they truly need and want help.

Ego has been the downfall of many. Ego is strong, powerful, and sneaky. When you think it is in balance, it gains control of you once again. Respect its power and all that it has taught you. But now it is time for you to take back the power that is rightfully yours. Your personal recipe is in the process of conscious change.

Balancing Fear & Courage

*"Be comfortable in the midst of your discomfort.
Ask courage to guide you."*

Fear is fed by yellow energy; Courage is fed with maroon energy. Both Fear and Courage are important ingredients in your personal recipe. Fear balances Courage; Courage balances Fear.

Fear and Courage each have positive and negative qualities. Usually, you think of Fear only in negative terms and Courage only in positive terms. Yet, without Fear, Courage would be out of balance. Courage might persuade you to do some foolish things with potentially devastating consequences.

Consider some of the many positive ways that Fear helps maintain inner balance:

Fear reminds you to think before you act. Fear of failure, fear of injury, and fear of ridicule are all examples of thinking about the consequences of your decisions before you act upon them.

Fear holds you in the present moment. Fear helps you focus on what is happening in your life **right now**. Understanding the present is the first step to understand past and future trends.

Fear keeps you in your comfort zone. All people strive to be comfortable wherever they are, whatever they do. Fear helps you stay right where you are—safe, secure, and comfortable.

Fear maintains distance from Self, creating a natural layer of protection. Fear gives you permission not to rush into the depths of Self too fast. As you move within, you will discover positive and negative aspects of Self. Both can be equally frightening.

Fear maintains distance from others, helping you to proceed with caution. Fear tells you that others have the power to hurt. When you want to aggressively pursue a relationship, Fear slows you down. Fear tells you to find as many facts as possible so that you will not be hurt.

To maintain inner balance, Fear explains why you "should not" act. Then Courage explains why you "should" act. Fear tries to keep you in the status quo. Courage encourages you to move. **You** weigh the facts after listening to both sides. The final decision to remain in the status quo or move is yours. Every time you decide against movement when the timing is correct, you give power to Fear. In this way, Fear accumulates more and more power. Eventually, Fear begins creating sub-personalities.

The Sub-Personalities Of Fear

One of the first sub-personalities that Fear creates is Inflexibility. Inflexibility helps in the battle against movement. Inflexibility says that no matter what, hold your ground. Do not bend, do not flow, do not trust anyone or anything.

Control and Manipulation are additional sub-personalities of Fear. Control and Manipulation tell you that they will help you get what you want. Sometimes these powerful sub-personalities even say, "Manage everything you do and everyone you meet. Without your direct interference you will get nothing that you want."

"If you have fear of flying, drive everywhere. This way you can control the way you might die." Never mind that when your time to leave this reality comes, it does not matter if you are in a plane or a car.

If you fear that friends and family can get along without you, Control and Manipulation will teach you how to use emotional blackmail. They say, "You can get people to stay in your life. That is much better than loneliness. It does not matter if others get what they want. It only matters that you get what **you** want."

Control and Manipulation continue, "If you fear that your children will grow up to be independent and no longer need you, use Anger, Guilt, Judgment, and Criticism. If you do not control them in some way, they may gain control over their own lives. Then, they may not need you." Now, you confuse wanting to be needed with love.

"If you fear loneliness, we can show you how to bring whomever you want into your life," state Control and Manipulation. Do you believe that the only way to establish a relationship is to manipulate your way into one?

"If you fear your companion will leave you," Control and Manipulation add, "we will help you out." However, is it possible that there may be someone better out there waiting for you to be available if he/she does leave?

If you fear that you will not get the job you want, Control and Manipulation will do their best to help you get it. But remember, you may be ignoring the possibility that something better may be just around the corner.

You may even fear that you are not good enough for positive experiences. Control and Manipulation will help keep positive experiences out of your life. Believe it or not, many people actively do their best to avoid allowing positive experiences into their lives. On some level of awareness, you may truly believe that "Good things happen to others, not to me." Walk through your fear of the positive.

Taking Power From Others

Whenever you allow Control and Manipulation to bring what you **want**, you ignore what you **need**. In addition, you take power away from others. You ask them to be who **you** want them to be; to do what **you** want them to do. You ask them to give up **their needs** and replace them with **your wants**. On some level of awareness, those people will resent this.

Allow others the freedom to be who they are, go where they want, select their own companions. Release your hold on them. The more freedom that you give to others, the more freedom you have to be who you are, go where you want, and select your own companions. This is because you walk through your own fear of finding out who **you** really are. Leniency with others means leniency with Self.

Allow others to move on with their lives. This may mean that they leave your life altogether. Or, it may allow them to grow into your life at a speed that **they** can handle. This allows you to take the power out of Control, Manipulation, and Fear. Instead, you give the power to your Oversoul and God-Mind, allowing them to bring the best people and situations into your life.

In essence, you take control long enough to hand that control up to your Oversoul and God-Mind. You still state what you want and why, yet you let them make the final decision. Then you accept that decision, always asking for explanation. By releasing others from your bondage, you not only free them and Self, but you give the freedom to your Oversoul and God-Mind to work in and through your life.

Each person has an Oversoul. His/her Oversoul is responsible for bringing the experiences that each needs. Trust each person to the care of his/her Oversoul. Via the involved Oversouls, ask that each person be brought the best experiences possible for his/her growth. Remember that every experience provides balance and growth, regardless of how painful or traumatic it appears. Nothing happens to anyone without agreement on the inner levels.

Ask that others be given the strength, knowledge, and wisdom to learn and grow in the best way for them. You cannot see or know everything about someone else. You have too much to learn about Self. Let each person's Oversoul do what is necessary without interference that will have repercussions at another time.

Recognize that your past actions are simply past actions. You did the best that you could with the knowledge that you had. You may wish to apologize to others or to Self via the involved Oversouls for past actions. If you feel any harshness towards Self for what you did, simply acknowledge these feelings. Release everything up to your Oversoul.

Fear Of Personal Power

You may be extremely afraid of your own personal power. Fear out of balance pulls your attention horizontally. When you walk **through** Fear, you move vertically. The more Fear you release, the deeper into your center you will go. Within these depths you access your personal power, melding Self with Oversoul and God-Mind. Once you access this power, then you have a new set of questions to answer:

What will I do with this personal power?

Will I control it or will it control me?

With additional personal power, what kind of knowledge will become available?

What will I do with the knowledge?

How will I handle the responsibility that comes with knowledge?

Will Ego grow out of control?

Now that I am stronger, what kind of negatives will I face?

Will I be able to handle positive growth experiences?

How will this personal power change my life?

Who and what will drop out of my life?

Who and what will move into my life?

Will I be able to let go of all that is no longer necessary?

Personal power means that your life as you know it will change. Knowledge brings responsibility and growth in a variety of ways. Are you willing to accept the challenge that your personal power offers?

Other Sub-Personalities Of Fear

Fear also creates other sub-personalities. Some of the most common include Insecurity, Nervousness, Anxiety, and Worry.

These sub-personalities collectively say:

I fear that I am not good enough.

I fear that I will be unable to live up to my own expectations.

I fear that others will not accept me as I am.

I fear that I will not be able to accomplish all that is necessary before the day is over.

I fear that I will not be able to make the correct decision.

I fear the past, present, and/or future.

The energy of these sub-personalities collectively feeds Stress.

Stress

Stress is well-fed from many lifelines, and is an important ingredient in your personal recipe. When Stress is in balance, it helps you realize the importance of getting things done in a timely, efficient manner. When Stress is out of balance, it puts excess pressure on you that you do not need.

Stress is dark, heavy yellow that it almost appears black. The energy of Stress is heavy, and leaves a residue similar to sand in your aura and body. This sand is an irritant that rubs on your protective nerve sheaths. Rubbing first in your auric field, it eventually works its way into your physical body. In this way, you create a negative nervous system.

Because Stress gains its strength gradually, you may become unaware of all the ways that it affects your body. Develop an awareness for the ways that Stress expresses in your body, such as:

Clenched fists, toes, and/or jaws.

Shoulders that hug your ears.

Shortness of breath.

Lower back tension.

Leg tension.

Tearing at your fingernails.

Check your body for Stress. Consciously relax the physical muscles that hold Stress. Then release the resulting residue up to your Oversoul. With your mind, will it out of your aura and body. Notice that Stress even expresses through your body while you sleep. Check your body for Stress when you retire at night. Take a moment to release it to allow for more restful sleep.

Choose to bring Stress into balance now. Be proactive. Do your best to allow at least thirty minutes every day just for yourself. Massage helps to break up the Stress that has already settled into your body. Ask a friend, partner, or spouse to massage the stress-filled parts of your body. Or, treat yourself to a professional massage with a licensed practitioner.

People often wait until illness sets in before they take care of their bodies. Although this is reactive, many people prefer this avenue of action. Only through the justification of illness do some people feel that they have a reason to spend time, energy, and money on Self and body.

Realize that you are special. You deserve to pamper Self and body right now. Rather than wait for Stress out of balance to teach you, practice preventive maintenance now.

Fear Is Normal

Know that it is perfectly normal to feel Fear. Fear is a natural part of the growth process. Releasing the known for the unknown can be frightening. Instead of saying "I shouldn't feel this way," simply acknowledge that you do. Take a deep breath. Then, recognizing that you are afraid, walk through Fear. Ask Courage to help pull you through, as it has been there all along, waiting for you to recognize and use it.

As you move through Fear, send the excess yellow energy of Fear out through the top of your head, up to your Oversoul. Ask your Oversoul to take all that you no longer need. Ask your Oversoul to strengthen Courage so that it, too, may come into balance. Measure your progress by your reactions. Compare your reactions of today versus your reactions of the past. Acknowledge your growth.

Make a conscious commitment to take care of your Fear before it takes care of you. This means learn about water through the enjoyment of swimming rather than through the fear of drowning. Learn about heights by skiing rather than by falling off a cliff. Be proactive. Move through Fear while you are strong, capable, and aware of what is happening rather than waiting until your defenses are down.

Bring Fear into balance gradually. Start on a small scale. If you are afraid of water, stand in shallow water. If standing in shallow water is too threatening, stand beside the shallow water. Take small steps in ways that you can handle.

Realize how many ways that Fear controls you. Look for the most mundane ways that Fear is in control. Start there. This is a beginning point that you can handle. One step at a time. There is no need to rush. Know that it is acceptable to be afraid and uncomfortable. Be comfortable in the midst of your discomfort. Ask Courage to guide you.

Fear out of balance paralyzes your life. The sub-personality becomes dense and heavy, living deep within Self and body. Fear out of balance clouds your vision and muddies your aura, and takes up space that belongs to Courage. You are special. You are important. You deserve to claim your potential. Make a conscious decision to bring Fear and Courage into their proper balance. Ask your Oversoul for guidance. Then begin the process.

BALANCING THE POSTIVES

*"All postive sub-personalities have
negative qualities as well."*

Most positive sub-personalities are generally thought of as "good." This allows them to quietly gather enough strength to push you out of your center and take control. Their strength is often underestimated because they are so widely accepted as "good." As with all things, positive sub-personalities are neither "good" nor "bad," but neutral. They have both positive and negative qualities.

Consider some of the following sub-personalities that are usually labeled "positive":

Trust

Love

Compassion

Honesty

Kindness

Prosperity

Happiness

Peace

Contentment

All of these sub-personalities have negative qualities, as well.

Trust

When Trust is too strong it lets others take advantage of you. Trust tells you that everyone is trustworthy. A casual stranger looks like a nice person. Trust says, "Here's a new friend." The other sub-personalities try to caution you, "People are not always what they first appear to be." You cannot hear this warning when Trust is too strong. If this person hurts you emotionally and/or physically, you wonder why. He/she seemed so nice.

Whenever anyone wants anything from you, Trust says, "Go ahead, he/she will pay you back/return it in good condition/not lose it." When people do not do as they say, you feel violated. Con artists love people with Trust that is too strong. When Trust is in balance, no one can take advantage of you.

Love

When Love is too strong, you can lose your personal identity. People often give their heart and soul to lovers, spouses, children, places, ideas, ideals, occupations. When this happens, these same people, places, and things control **you**. **You** lose your power.

Think about Love of alcohol, Love of gambling, Love of food, Love of money, Love of power, Love of sports, Love of work, Love of play. The list can go on forever. In balance, these Loves are wonderful additions to your personal recipe. Out of balance, these Loves consume the real you.

Love out of balance even causes people to kill: Love of a spouse, child, lover. People go to war for Love of ideas, Love of a nation. Balanced Love means that it is a part of you but it does not control you.

Compassion

When Compassion becomes too strong, living in this world can be difficult. When you see poverty, hunger, pain, and suffering, how can you live with yourself? You have shelter, food, adequate healthcare, plus. How can you enjoy life when so many people do not have the basic necessities of life? When Compassion is too strong, you may have trouble sleeping at night—the Compassion you feel may be overwhelming. On the other hand, a Compassion that is too weak creates a heart that is cold and unemotional.

Compassion in balance tells you that there are reasons why these people chose these life circumstances. The reasons may or may not be important for you to know. Compassion in balance keeps your heart open with an appreciation for the struggles of others. Compassion in balance also lets other sub-personalities explain your options— what kind of help you can offer without interfering in others' lessons while at the same time maintaining your own needs.

Honesty

When Honesty is too strong, you may lose your personal privacy. Some people ask all kinds of invasive questions. You are not under any obligation to answer prying questions. You may tell the rest of the world only what you wish. You are only accountable to Self, Oversoul, and God-Mind.

Persons traveling alone must be cautious. An innocent remark from an honest person can put personal safety in jeopardy. Parents teach their children not to talk to strangers. Privacy must be protected for a variety of reasons. You can be too honest.

Kindness

You can even be too kind. When Kindness is too strong you may ignore the **needs** of others. You forget that what a person **needs** is often different from what he/she wants. Kindness tells you to give to others what he/she wants; perhaps even what **you** want for another. Many people need pain, suffering, and struggles. Without these, they would not have the impetus to grow. If you are too kind, they may never acquire the strength and growth that they need from their hardships.

In addition, Oversouls spend a great deal of time preparing specific situations for specific individuals. If you remove this situation by alleviating the hardship, the person's Oversoul must start over to re-create what you have unknowingly dismantled in your "kindness." Remember that even though a test is difficult, each individual must pass his/her own test. When you take someone else's test, you are the only one that learns.

Too much kindness sometimes destroys relationships. There are many people who return acts of kindness with suspicion and distrust. Some people feel unworthy of kindness. The more kindness they receive, the faster they run in the opposite direction. There are some people who will never be able to accept kindness. Only through inner communication with your Oversoul can you truly determine how much kindness another is able to accept and you are allowed to give.

Abundance

What happens when Abundance is too strong? Without proper balance from other sub-personalities, Abundance brings its own challenges. Responsibility, Self-Esteem, Ego, and Guilt are only a few of the sub-personalities that must be reasonably balanced. You must be able to manage Abundance; to feel worthy of abundance; to recognize that Abundance is a part of you but is not you; and to accept Abundance for Self, knowing that many others exist in a deficit position.

The news media present numerous stories about people who suddenly find themselves in a lucrative financial position. Some handle this quite well. Yet, there are many who cannot justify this type of abundance in their lives. One way or another, they find ways to relieve themselves of the funds. When Abundance grows too quickly, some people do not have the proper balance to handle it.

Peace

When Peace is too strong, it may lead you into a dull and boring life. Most people need a certain amount of outside stimuli to keep themselves interested in living. Life emulates art when you realize how quickly action characters in theater or television captivate an audience's attention. Without activity, the audience becomes bored. This is true in life. People enjoy activity. With awareness, do your best to bring balanced activity into your life.

Contentment

An overabundance of contentment leads to laziness. When everything is in its place, you become complacent. Life is going well, so why disturb it? Why not remain on a plateau forever? To do nothing seems like the easiest path. However, everything can always be better. Nothing ever remains the same. If you do not continually move, something will happen to move you. Do your best to be proactive. Strive on your own to make a good life even better.

Happiness

When Happiness grows too strong, you may lose touch with the realities of life. Because you do not struggle, you may forget that others do struggle. Sometimes a callous attitude develops that says, "If I can be happy, why can't you?"

You may forget that you are not on this Earth alone. When you acquire Happiness, it is probably because somewhere along the way, someone paid attention to your struggles. Either on the seen or unseen levels, someone stopped his/her journey long enough to help you. Now it is your turn to stop for a moment and return the favor by helping someone else.

Why Do "Nice Guys Finish Last?"

Almost everyone has known someone who was a "really nice guy" who always seemed to have bad luck. After observing this person with all of these admirable qualities, it becomes puzzling. If he is as wonderful as he appears, why does he continually attract such bad luck?

You are merely a witness to the process of balance. These people have positive sub-personalities that are much too strong. As a result, they attract negative experiences that try to strengthen their negative sub-personalities. Negative sub-personalities are needed to function in everyday life.

Eventually, positive sub-personalities must weaken while negative sub-personalities must strengthen for a "nice guy" to survive. One way or another, these people will learn that there are positive reasons for the existence of negative sub-personalities.

Always remember that negative sub-personalities are not "bad." Negative sub-personalities exist to balance positive sub-personalities. Positive sub-personalities are not better than negative sub-personalities. All sub-personalities are necessary to keep your personal recipe in a position of neutrality.

As a microcosm of the macrocosm, your microcosm constantly strives to emulate the neutrality of the macrocosm. You, your Oversoul, and God-Mind are all neutral energy. On some level of awareness, your microcosm knows that. In its own way it does its best to maintain your overall personality in a neutral state. If it sees a (-3), (-5), and a (-8), it does its best to add a (+16) in any way possible so that the personality maintains its overall position of neutrality.

Cultivate Inner Awareness

Cultivate an inner awareness that explains how specific sub-personalities balance each other. The following list provides examples of sub-personalities that balance each other:

Trust/Distrust;

Love/Logic;

Compassion/Harshness;

Honesty/Dishonesty;

Kindness/Unkindness;

Abundance/Lack;

Peace/Activity;

Contentment/Growth;

and,

Happiness/Unhappiness.

All sub-personalities are important to maintain inner balance.

Too Strong

When positive sub-personalities are too strong, ask your Oversoul to take all the energy of that particular sub-personality. Ask it to give back only what you need. Notice the color of the sub-personality that is too strong. With your mind, will that colored energy out of your aura, up to your Oversoul.

Too Weak

When sub-personalities are too weak, use affirmations and visualization techniques to increase their energy. Recognize that your negative sub-personalities may try to sabotage your work. The more you try, the more resistance you may feel. When this happens, remember that **you** are in control. You are in the process of taking back your personal power.

Negative sub-personalities may do their best to maintain the control to which they are accustomed. They may remind you of how much you learn through negative experiences. For instance, Illness, Discomfort, and Pain teach you how to care for and appreciate your body. Stress forces you to find Calm. Unhappiness motivates you to search for Happiness.

Negative sub-personalities may trick you into believing that you deserve these negative experiences. After all, you expect trauma to infiltrate your life. When you are fortunate enough to have positive experiences, it is your too-strong negative sub-personalities that say:

Enjoy it while it's here; it won't last long!

This is too good to be true!

Your life is too smooth; what is going to happen next?

Everything is going too well; what awaits you around the next corner?

These negative sub-personalities keep weak positive sub-personalities weak. They tell you that it is only negative growth experiences that move you toward your Oversoul and God-Mind; you need them to grow; without them you will stagnate and die. These negative sub-personalities do not want to relinquish control. Because you have done so in your past, it is easy to listen to these sub-personalities. You relied on these negative sub-personalities to help you grow. You spent many lifelines listening to and feeding these negative sub-personalities.

Now you can acknowledge the importance of all sub-personalities. You can address each one individually, or as a group. As you take control, explain how important each one has been, is, and always will be to your personal recipe. Thank each one for its continuing service. Explain that **you** are now in control. **You** are captain of your team. Under the guidance of your Oversoul and God-Mind, continue to meld all parts of Self into a comfortable level of inner balance.

THE REST OF THE RAINBOW

*"Consciously choose the colors that best promote the personality
that you are in the process of creating."*

Identifying the colors of your sub-personalities gives you increasing control over what you do or do not want in your personal recipe. Your knowledge of color allows you to target specific sub-personalities for either strengthening or weakening. You strengthen a sub-personality by directing additional colored energy into it. You weaken a sub-personality by draining excess colored energy from it.

All sub-personalities are necessary. Each contributes something to the whole. You never eliminate any of them. You only give back to your Oversoul all that you no longer need.

As a general rule, when there is excess energy in a sub-personality, that sub-personality becomes dark and heavy. As the sub-personalities comes into balance, the color changes to clear and light. Each sub-personality has a specific shade of color. All sub-personalities have both positive and negative qualities. Use the following information as a guideline to delve deeper into your own personal recipe. Ask your Oversoul for direction, remembering that each individual is unique.

Green

Depending upon the shade, green energy strengthens Jealousy, Greed, Lack, Illness, Health, Contentment, Abundance, Generosity. Jealousy forces you to observe other people; motivates you into action; helps set priorities. Contentment balances Jealousy. Greed balances Generosity. Illness balances Health. Lack balances Prosperity.

Blue

Blue energy strengthens Communication, Depression, Ignorance, Deceit, Peacefulness, Calmness, Serenity, Concentration, Clarity. Lack of the corresponding color of blue restricts your ability to communicate; an overabundance may mean a constant stream of chatter pours from your mouth. Depression is balanced by Peacefulness, Calmness, and Serenity. Ignorance balances Knowledge. Deceit balances Truth.

Violet

Violet strengthens the sub-personalities called Selfishness and Selflessness. Selfishness is an important sub-personality. Selfishness teaches you to think about yourself; to become strong and feel good about who you are and what you deserve. When Selfishness is too strong you forget that anyone else exists.

Selflessness balances Selfishness. Selflessness reminds you that you live amongst other people with needs similar to your own. However, when Selflessness is too strong, you do so much for others that you do not have the time to take care of Self. When this happens, Resentment and Bitterness grow. So, Selfishness is necessary to balance Selflessness.

Using The Colors

Apply your knowledge of color to the following basic universal laws:

1. The outer world always reflects the inner world.

2. The inner world always reflects the outer world.

Because of this law, you can effectively make extensive inner changes through the use of color in your environment.

Color does one of three things:

• Holds you where you are.

• Pulls you into your past.

• Elevates you up into your potential.

Holds You Where You Are

The colors that you choose can hold you where you are. If, for example, you know that Resentment is too strong, take a look around you. You may be surprised at how much of that color of red is in your environment. When you use that color to decorate your home, office, car, or body (clothing, jewelry), the red energy of Resentment automatically pulls out toward that color.

Regardless of how much you try to pull Resentment into center, you fight the pull of the red energy in your environment. Resentment wants to express, and uses the appropriate shade of red in the environment to add strength to itself. Adding more of that shade of red continues to hold you where you are.

Eliminating that shade of red eliminates its anchor in the outer world. When you will it into your center, you take back your power. This action says, "You can no longer control me." Once you pull Resentment into your center, pass up to your Oversoul all that you no longer need.

Into Your Past

Color can also pull you into your past. If you have moved through Depression but still have a tendency to be depressed, choose to remove the color that makes you "feel blue."

Sometimes any dark, heavy color may make you feel depressed. Be aware of which colors these are so that you can avoid them until Depression is in better balance. Choose to use colors that hold you where you want to be while you stabilize the "new" personality.

Into Your Potential

To strengthen sub-personalities, decorate your environment with colors that express the sub-personalities that you want drawn out. You may choose clear, clean reds to promote Creativity; clear, clean greens to foster Health, Abundance, and emotional stability; pinks for Love and Compassion; sparkling golds to draw out inner Wisdom. Understanding the colors of specific sub-personalities allows you to make better conscious choices.

Choose The Best For You

Consciously choose the colors that best promote the personality that you are in the process of creating. On some level of awareness, you already choose colors, designs, and patterns. Bring that knowledge forward into your conscious mind to be the most effective co-creator of Self. The following information will help you choose the best colors for your environment to accomplish your personal goals. These are only guidelines. Always ask your Oversoul to help you make your own individual choice.

Guidelines For Color

Avoid reds as you weaken the sub-personalities of Anger, Bitterness, Hate, and/or Resentment. Red is also the color of Sexuality. Use reds to strengthen that sub-personality or to weaken it, depending upon your needs. Creativity is fostered by clear, clean reds.

Pinks bring Love and Compassion into expression. Add rose quartz to your environment—stones, jewelry, bookends, etc.—to pull these sub-personalities into full expression. Avoid them to weaken these sub-personalities.

Use orange to strengthen Self-Esteem and Ego. As Self Esteem strengthens and Ego comes into balance, you will be more comfortable with peach tones in your environment. Orange is also the color of psychic energy. Psychic energy is your personal energy. When you give away too much psychic energy, orange will replenish that energy for you.

Yellow energy strengthens Logic, Wisdom, Knowledge, Intellect, Courage, and Fear. Eliminate yellows for awhile to deflate Logic that is too strong. Add yellows for the opposite effect. Take into account the other sub-personalities strengthened by yellow to determine which shade of yellow has either a positive or negative effect on Self. Choose the shades you need for balance.

Gold is a catalyst that pulls out inner wisdom. Gold metal is solidifying. Wearing gold around your neck helps you remain centered. When you know a challenging situation with challenging people is coming up, wear gold to help keep yourself centered. Avoid gold if you have a tendency to be inflexible.

Use bright, clear greens to strengthen Health, Abundance, Contentment, and Generosity. Greens heals emotions, oxygenates the entire physical system, and strengthens the heart and lungs. Green plants are a wonderful addition to any home or office space. When you want to weaken Jealousy, Greed, Lack, or Illness, avoid dark, heavy greens.

Dark, heavy blues strengthen Depression. Light, clear blues strengthen Peace, Calm, and Serenity. Ice blue strengthens communication. Royal blue strengthens Clarity and Concentration.

The absence or addition of violets and purples strengthens or weakens Selfishness or Selflessness, depending upon your goal. Muddy violets and purples strengthen Selfishness, clear violets and purples strengthen Selflessness.

White is a cleansing color. White will irritate a delicate nervous system. If your job requires you to wear white, you may choose to wear a layer of underclothing in soft colors to help protect the nervous system. Only choose white if you have a strong constitution. Cream (white plus gold) is a softer color and easier on the nervous system.

Black is sometimes thought of as a negative color. Many negative sub-personalities contain some black. Whenever you weaken any heavy aspect of Self, you may wish to avoid black. As with all things, black has many positive qualities. Black is an insulating, protective, depth color; it also allows you to remain hidden, mysterious, and secretive. Using black calls for a strong constitution so that you use it without allowing it to use you.

Gray strengthens Change, Flexibility, and Movement. Gray can also add to confusion. Avoid gray if you have difficulty remaining in your center, or if you just feel like you need to stand still and catch your breath. Silver strengthens Change, Flexibility, and Movement. It also helps you connect to your Oversoul level.

Brown strengthens Stability and Stagnation. Browns foster your connection to the Earth and nature. Use brown to ground yourself. If your tendency is to complain, do nothing, and stagnate, avoid browns.

Use Design For Growth

The way that you use particular designs promotes or inhibits growth. Develop your awareness of the many ways to use design to pull yourself up into your potential.

Solid colors pull you into your center. Wear solid colors in challenging situations to avoid being pulled "off-center." Solid colors can also have a calming, quieting effect on your environment. Avoid solids if you have a tendency to be stagnant and/or inflexible.

Busy patterns are great for play and activity. They break up inflexibility as well as old routines. If remaining centered is a challenge for you, avoid busy patterns—they can scatter your energy. If you like patterns around you, remember that smaller patterns keep your energy closer to center, while larger patterns help break up tendencies to be inflexible. Floral patterns allow you to bloom.

Horizontal stripes are not for people who have difficulty making decisions. Stripes that run this direction keep you running around in circles. However, if you are on vacation and prefer not to think about anything, horizontal stripes will help you delay making decisions. Vertical stripes move your energy up and down, aligning it with universal energy.

Polka dots usually represent holes in the aura. Ask your Oversoul to heal these holes which are often the result of harsh or bitter words. Polka dots can also represent a sparkling inner light trying to express. If this is so, ask your Oversoul to remove any obstacles that prevent your inner light from full expression.

Dark colors ground Self into the logical portion of your mind. Dark colors are great for business meetings or any event where your mind has a tendency to wander. Conversely, light colors allow you to drift into your emotional side. Before you choose light colors, decide if you need more or less "drifting" in your life.

Simultaneous Lives

People often choose colors and/or designs that are indicative of simultaneous lives. Former prisoners often find comfort in stripes. Or, people who feel like prisoners in this lifeline also wear stripes. Wearing black in this lifeline may remind you of the comfort you felt in a nunnery or a lifeline as a black magician. Someone who had a beautiful flower garden, or who wished for one, may choose to surround him/herself with an abundance of floral patterns.

Often people choose colors that were predominant in a lifeline that they particularly enjoyed or disliked. People often fill their environment with designs or objects from other cultures. Why do you choose one culture over another? These are clues from other lifelines. Investigate them.

Words

In **Section II**, the chapter *What Did You Say?* Explained about the color of words. Now that you know more about color, continue to observe the color of the words that you speak. Recognize that words spoken in anger use red energy. Words spoken in compassion use pink energy. Lies are black with holes. Knowledge is yellow. Observe the color of the energy that you feel behind the following affirmations:

God-Mind wisdom directs me.

God-Mind peace permeates me.

God-Mind love moves in and through me.

Feel the gold in the first statement, blue in the second, and pink in the last. Observe your words. Be aware of the color of energy that you use. Choose to use colors that promote harmony and balance within Self.

221

Food

Even the foods that you eat strengthen the energy of specific sub-personalities. Be aware of the color of the food that you put into your body. Understand the feeling behind the type of food that you choose. Does it feel nutritious and body-building? Does it help or hinder personal growth?

Observe that foods with high acidity break down the rubbery energy of Guilt. Cold, clammy foods strengthen Fear, yet may cool hot temperaments. Hot, spicy foods fuel Anger, yet break down Fear. Greens oxygenate the entire system. Observe the effects of specific foods upon your overall personality.

Observe which foods make you feel whole and healthy. Notice the colors of foods that you choose. Choose foods that nurture not only the physical self, but also the mental, emotional, and spiritual parts of Self.

You Are Unique

Because each individual is unique, use the above information as a guideline to direct your learning. The same color, design, or food may affect two people differently depending upon the personal recipe of each individual. This information is only a starting point. Always ask your Oversoul for guidance and clarification so that your observations of Self and others can be as accurate as possible. And finally, always give thanks for the answers that you receive.

KNOW YOUR AURA

*"Because the outer always reflects the inner, all you have to do is survey
your environment to learn about your aura contents."*

You may think that you must be a "psychic" to know the contents of your aura. As previously discussed, a "psychic" is only aware of conditions that already exist. On some level of awareness you already know everything that there is to know about your aura. All you have to do is bring that awareness forward into your conscious mind.

This is really very easy. Ask your Oversoul to show you what you need to know about your aura. Answers usually come within seconds from the level of knowing. Logic may try to reason you out of your answer. Logic may tell you that this process should be much more difficult. If you listen to Logic you may get stuck in the level of guessing. Do your best to stay in the level of knowing.

Because all "seeing" occurs in the mind anyway, it does not matter whether you look at your aura with your eyes open or closed. As you read this chapter, simply glance at your aura whenever it is appropriate.

Create Boundaries

Observe how far from your body your aura extends. Observe its shape. With your mind, will your aura to move in two to three feet from your body. You will your physical body to move all the time. You will your arms to raise, and they do. You will your legs to walk, and they do. You will your eyes to open and close. In the same way, will your aura to move. Your mind is a powerful tool.

Now, will a violet bubble around your aura. Ask your Oversoul to send energy that you may use to create a bubble that encases your aura. Your mind quickly manipulates this energy to form the bubble. As fast as you think, you create. Your mind wills this bubble into existence. On some level of awareness, it can be seen. This bubble sets the boundaries of Self—where you start and stop. Boundaries are important to keep yourself clean and free from psychic debris.

Observe The Contents

Observe where your aura is light and where it is dark. Are the light places positives or negatives? Are the dark places positives or negatives? What colors would you like to move out of your aura? What colors would you like to make stronger or brighter?

Are Logic and Emotion in balance? Logic is yellow, Emotion is green. Do you have equal parts of each, or is one stronger than the other? Are there any other specific colors that you notice?

Does your aura have any holes or webs? Does it contain any particular patterns? Do you have any interesting symbols in your aura? If so, what do these mean? Are they a part of your past, present, future, or of all three?

Does your aura have an identifiable center? Is it aligned along your spine? Is your center flexible and strong, or inflexible and brittle? Is your center connected to and/or melded with your Oversoul and God-Mind? If you do not have an identifiable center, review the meditation chapter, *Into the Silence* in **Section 1** for tools to create your center.

Are your chakra bands in the proper sequence? Do they spin or are they stagnant? If they spin, do they spin in the same direction? Are they clean and clear? The breathing work that you do during meditation automatically aligns and cleanses your chakras for you.

Psychic Cords

Notice if you have any psychic cords that extend beyond your bubble. These cords actually exist. Every time someone has a thought about you, the energy of that thought heads off in your direction. The more times someone thinks about you, the stronger the cord becomes. The energy accumulates with each thought until eventually the cord reaches you and grabs on.

In the same way, every time you think about someone the energy of your thoughts heads off in his/her direction. This is why it is so important that you send the energy of your thoughts up to your Oversoul as you think. This stops any unnecessary psychic cords from building.

Psychic cords can extend from you to another person, animal, place, or thing, or vice versa, regardless if you know who or what is on the other end. If you see or feel any cords, ask your Oversoul to resolve any unnecessary psychic ties on the inner levels. Ask it to dissipate the corresponding psychic cords on the Oversoul level, and that the energies that created these be returned to their correct owners. Also ask for information on any necessary psychic cords that remain. Send your thoughts up to your Oversoul to prevent additional psychic cords from establishing themselves where they are not necessary.

Consciously Create

Using the power of your mind, you can consciously create your aura any way you desire so long as your wishes coincide with the wishes of your Oversoul. You already

unconsciously create your aura every second of every day. Awareness gives you the opportunity to know what it is that you create at the moment of creation. This means that you can make immediate changes if you choose.

Every aura is comprised of many layers. The outer layers generally are an expression of this moment in time. This is one reason why aura colors can be different at any given time. A person's true aura colors are often buried in the innermost layers.

Once you recognize how easy it is to know your own aura, your awareness of others' auras increases. Remember that you already see auras. Now you are only becoming aware of what already exists. Never pry into anyone else's space. You would not want someone prying into your space. Instead, ask your Oversoul to show you whatever it is that you **need**, not **want**, to know whenever you meet someone.

Layers Of Auras

The concept of the layers of auras is particularly important when dealing with other people. For instance, a positive person may have a dark, foreboding outer aura layer because he/she may be doing some intense internal housecleaning. If you look at this outer layer without asking your Oversoul for explanation, you may mislabel this person "negative."

In the same way, a negative person who knows the laws can consciously create a beautiful aura by willing all dark, foreboding colors and symbols into his/her innermost layers. If you look at this outer layer without asking your Oversoul for explanation, you may mislabel this person "positive." Developing inner communication allows you to have a reliable source of information available when you need it. Constantly continue to cultivate your relationship with your Oversoul and God-Mind.

Ask your Oversoul to help determine how much of each sub-personality is needed for your personal recipe. Do this by willing the entire sub-personality up to your Oversoul. Then ask your Oversoul to return the sub-personality in a form that matches your current level of development.

Know Your Aura

You always know exactly what is in your aura. You are merely developing your awareness of what already exists. Because the outer always reflects the inner, all you have to do is survey your environment to learn about your aura contents.

Look around the area that you are in right now. Use color, design, lightness, darkness, cultural influence, symbols, and objects as clues. Whatever surrounds you in the outer world always reflects your aura. Determine for yourself how easy it is to develop conscious awareness of your aura contents.

You can never be in any place that does not reflect your aura. Even if you want to go to a particular place, you will not be able to get there if it does not reflect your aura. Or, you may find yourself in a place that you would rather not be because this place reflects your aura in some way. As long as you remember that the outer always reflects the inner and the inner always reflects the outer, you will continue to develop conscious awareness of the contents of your aura.

WAKING UP

"You remember that you are here as an extension of God-Mind; to help God-Mind experience God-Mind; to help God-Mindexplain God-Mind."

Waking up each morning often brings memories of dreams from the previous night. Sometimes you remember dreams right away; sometimes they pop into your head several days later. Some dreams you remember from beginning to end, some only bits and pieces. Remembering dreams requires a conscious desire to bring subconscious activity forward into your conscious mind.

In the same way, self-awareness simply means waking up to your own part of the cosmic dream. Self-knowledge is part of the waking-up process. This is almost as though you are in the midst of a dream. Every time you reach inside you bring more and more of that dream forward into your conscious mind. **You know that you already know**. Each piece of knowledge that you access makes you remember that there is something else to remember. You are in the process of waking up to your true identity.

As a microcosm of the macrocosm, you are a replica in miniature of God-Mind. **God-Mind is neither positive nor negative, but contains both**. God-Mind expresses itself through your sub-personalities. Each sub-personality is an expression of God-Mind. Each one is important to the whole. As you acknowledge and understand these parts of Self, you also have greater knowledge and understanding of God-Mind.

You are not in the process of eliminating any of your sub-personalities. Each one is an important part of the whole. You are, however, in the process of bringing them into balance to replicate the balance of God-Mind.

Remember Your True Purpose

You are waking up, or remembering, your true purpose. You remember that you are here as an extension of God-Mind; to help God-Mind experience God-Mind; to help God-Mind explain God-Mind. Your sub-personalities are an aid in the process. They are under the sole direction of your Oversoul until you become conscious enough to take control. Once you take control you work with your Oversoul to actively co-create your personal journey into God-Mind. The more details about Self that you remember, the better you become as an active partner in your journey.

Every experience that occurs has an order; experiences do not happen randomly. This order continually brings balance to any part of Self that becomes unbalanced. God-Mind must always be in balance. Likewise, your internal structure must always be in balance to maintain a level of inner comfort. Regardless of the experience, always ask:

Which sub-personality(ies) did this experience nudge closer toward balance?

Did a particularly embarrassing moment help to deflate Ego?

Were you taken advantage of because Trust is too strong?

Did you have an accident because Anger needs to be dissipated?

Did you provide someone with gossip about yourself because Honesty is out of balance?

Did something get taken away from you because Jealousy needs weakening?

Just as God-Mind always maintains a neutral state, so do you. Sub-personalities consistently strive to make this happen. In-depth knowledge of your sub-personalities allows you to decide in conjunction with your Oversoul how to maintain a neutral state in the most effective, pleasant, and least painful way.

Knowledge Gives Choices

Knowledge gives a person choices. Knowledge of this ongoing process of inner balance allows you to make choices that lead to inner peace and contentment. You even develop a degree of comfort with uncomfortable choices when you understand that they are designed to bring some part of Self into balance.

Section III includes knowledge that gives you additional choices. You now have tools to help you:

Take back your power.

Be proactive.

Understand your personal recipe.

Strengthen/weaken sub-personalities.

Create with color.

Balance positives with negatives.

Balance negatives with positives.

Know the contents of your aura.

Become an active, conscious co-creator of your journey.

Use the tools you now have available to accomplish your goals in conscious awareness. Understand that how deep you go and how fast you get there depends on the overall balance of Self. Your Oversoul will only let you travel inward at a rate that all sub-personalities can handle. You can always ask for faster travel, but listen to the wisdom of your Oversoul. Understand as well as accept the experiences that you are given as necessary for inner balance. Allow yourself to wake up at a rate that you can comfortably handle.

Some of your sub-personalities may come into balance very quickly; others may take lifelines. The process is unique for each individual. As you continue to develop conscious awareness of your personal process, enjoy the wonder of self-exploration, knowing that exploration of Self is exploration of God-Mind.

Enjoy the process.

APPENDICES III

SOME THINGS TO TRY

IDENTIFY YOUR SUB-PERSONALITIES

Whenever you think, speak, or act, identify all the sub-personalities that are involved. When you think about helping another, for example, identify all the sub-personalities involved in the process:

Do you want to help because it will make you feel better (Ego)?

Or because this person truly needs and wants your help (Selflessness)?

Are words spoken in Anger laced with Resentment and Bitterness?

Is Jealousy involved in Happiness?

Observe the intent and motivation behind your actions:

Which sub-personalities are involved? for what reasons?

Observe when you are in control and when your sub-personalities are in control.

LOVE

Observe the actions of the people who say they love you:
   Do their actions match their words?
   Do you feel loved?
   Do you ever feel rebellious toward them?
   Do you feel like you must suppress your identity when you are around them?
   Is this love?

Observe your actions toward people whom you think you love:
   Do you think these people feel loved?
   Do your actions match your words?
   Are they ever rebellious toward you?
   Do they suppress their identity around you?
   Is this love?

POSITIVE GROWTH

Create a pattern of positive growth in your life. Do something positive for yourself today:

Buy yourself a plant or flowers.

Go for a walk.

Read something that makes you laugh.

Take an hour just for yourself.

Clean something that needs cleaning.

Take time to write your affirmations.

Meditate for five minutes.

Only accept positive internal self-talk.

Be around people who help pull you up into your potential.

PROACTIVE CHOICES

Think of a situation that you are avoiding. Do something about it today! Be proactive. Take control of the situation before it takes control of you.

"PREDICTING" THE FUTURE

Develop your ability to "predict" the future:

Before you telephone someone, ask your Oversoul if the energy was sent for him/her to receive the call.

Before you go shopping, ask if the energy was sent to help you find what you are looking for.

Before you attend a specific event, ask if the energy was sent for you to have an enjoyable time.

Simple exercises develop your ability to feel or see what does or does not already exist on the inner levels.

GUILT

Identify three situations in which someone makes you feel guilty. Observe:
    Why does he/she choose to make you feel guilt?
    Does he/she consciously realize how you feel?

Identify three situations in which you make another feel guilty. Observe:
    Why do you choose to make another feel guilty?
    How does this make you feel?
    How does the other person feel?
    Could you act in a different way to create a more positive influence in his/her life?

EGO & SELF-ESTEEM

How many different forms of excess ego can you identify within yourself? in others?

When has excess ego been helpful?

What can you do to increase your self-esteem?

POSITIVE SUB-PERSONALITIES

Observe your positive sub-personalities to find out if you have any that are too strong:

Are you ever too nice? too kind?

Do people take advantage of you?

Do you do so much for others that you and/or your immediate family suffer?

Do you say "yes" when you want to say "no?"

When do positive sub-personalities take control?

COLORS & DESIGNS

Observe the colors and designs with which you surround yourself:

Do you have an abundance of one color/design?

Why do you choose specific colors/designs? How do they make you feel? Do you like the way they make you feel?

What is your ideal color/design?

How can you achieve this in a simple way?

What sub-personalities do your colors/designs accentuate?

AFFIRMATIONS

Choose one or two of the following affirmations. Make any changes that personalize them for you. Think, say, or write them throughout your day. Use them to bring balance into your inner and outer worlds.

ABUNDANCE
I always have enough.
I am open and receptive to abundance.
I am worthy of abundance.
Abundance flows into every area of my life.
Abundance fills every area of my life.

AURA
I know the contents of my aura.
I choose the contents of my aura.
My Oversoul teaches me about the contents of my aura.
I feel the shape, color, consistency, and color of the energy within my aura.
I release any unnecessary psychic cords up to my Oversoul.
I release anything that I no longer need from my aura.
I keep my aura clean and clear.

BALANCE
I consciously recognize the process of balance.
I appreciate/respect the process of balance.
I finish the last act of the old script with appreciation and understanding.
I release any illusions that label the old script "bad."
I understand the full spectrum of every experience.
I change the outer world to change the inner world.
I change the inner world to change the outer world.
I allow the outer world to teach me about my past, present, and future.

CHALLENGING SITUATIONS
I allow my challenging situations to teach me.
I release the need for reactive learning.
I choose proactive learning.
I make proactive choices.
I allow myself to explore the challenging parts of Self.

COLORS
I appreciate the uniqueness of my personal color combination.
I release the excess color of too-strong sub-personalities up to my Oversoul.
I ask for additional color to strengthen too-weak sub-personalities.
I acknowledge the color of my words.
I observe the color of the foods that I choose.
I effectively use design and color to promote inner change.

CONSCIOUS AWARENESS

I know that I already know.
I create in conscious awareness.
I am a microcosm of the macrocosm.
Whatever is within me, is within God-Mind.
I share both positive and negative experiences with God-Mind.
I anchor myself in the strength of my Oversoul and God-Mind.
I remember my connection to my Oversoul and God-Mind.

EGO & SELF-ESTEEM

I accept myself as is.
I like myself even when I do not like myself.
I release the need to be the center of the universe.
My ego and self-esteem are in balance and harmony.

EMOTIONS

I allow myself to feel all my emotions.
All my emotions are valid.
I recognize any emotions that control me.
I release my need for excess negative emotions.
I release my need for excess positive emotions.
I allow myself to feel comfortable in the midst of my discomfort.

GUILT

I release any mind-patterns that create a need for guilt.
I release any people that I hold onto with guilt.
I release my need to control and manipulate others with guilt.
I release my need to be responsible for situations for which I am not responsible.
I release my need to judge/criticize Self/others.

RESPECT

I am worthy of respect.
I respect myself.
I respect others.
I respect the struggles of others.
I respect the uniqueness of each individual.

STRESS

I release the need for excess stress in my life.
I release the excess energy of stress up to my Oversoul.
I release excess stress from my physical body.
I consciously acknowledge all the ways that stress expresses
through my physical body.
I allow myself to relax and let go.

SUB -PERSONALITIES

I take back my personal power.
I take command of my team.
I acknowledge all sub-personalities.
I easily identify my sub-personalities.

I easily identify all sub-personalities that are too strong/weak.
I am a conscious co-creator of my emerging personality.
I am a conscious co-creator of my journey.
I release all that I no longer need up to my Oversoul.
I understand the positive aspects of my negative sub-personalities.
I understand the negative aspects of my positive sub-personalities.

MEDITATIONS

CONSCIOUS RELEASE OF EXCESS ENERGY

As you sit to meditate, focus your attention on all the sub-personalities that circle around the nucleus that is you. Begin your breathing work, as described in **Section I.** As you feel your breath pull you into your center, say the following to your Oversoul and God-Mind:

Thank you for all that I have and all that I receive. Thank you for the knowledge that allows me to understand myself. Because I am still learning about my sub-personalities, I ask you to take them all back and return only what I need.

(With your breath, push all that you contain out the top of your head and up to your Oversoul. Allow it to flow and flow. When you finish, allow your Oversoul to send back all that you need. Allow yourself to feel the calm, peace, and lightness that now surrounds you as a result of releasing the heaviness that you no longer need.)

Thank you for taking all that I no longer need. Thank you for giving me what I do need. Thank you for your personal instruction on my journey into Self, Oversoul, and God-Mind.

ACKNOWLEDGMENT OF SELF

Follow your breath into your center. Allow yourself to feel anchored in the strength of Self, Oversoul, and God-Mind. Know that anchored deep within your center, you can face any part of Self.

Feel that you are a part of God-Mind, a part of All That Is—all good, all bad; all positive, all negative. Breathe in, breathe out. Allow any part of Self that wants to, pass before your inner eye. Release any judgment or criticism toward this part of Self out the top of your head, up to your Oversoul and God-Mind.

Breathe in, breathe out. From your center, observe yourself as you feel the negative parts of Self. Observe either specific or general thoughts, or negative emotions. Give them color, weight, consistency. Notice whether they are dark or light; if they are solid or filled with holes. Release all of your observations up to your Oversoul.

Repeat to yourself: I love and approve of myself as is. All that I contain is important to who and what I am. I created myself in accordance with my Oversoul and God-Mind. I am neither positive nor negative, but contain both. Both are important to explain who and what I am, who and what my Oversoul is, and who and what God-Mind is. For this knowledge and understanding, I give thanks.

RECYCLING YOUR ENERGY

Any time that you wish, during meditation or throughout the day, breathe yourself into your center. Will all the excess energy of past and current experiences into your center. With your breath, push it out through the top of your head and up to your Oversoul. Silently say to your Oversoul and God-Mind: I return to you all that comes from you.

RELEASING ANGER

From your center, observe your sub-personality named Anger. Observe its color, shape, and density. Observe how heavy it makes you feel. With your mind, breathe it into your center.

Will all the excess energy that it contains to flow out the top of your head, up the channel to your Oversoul. Watch it flow and flow.

Feel yourself become lighter and cleaner as the excess energy leaves your personal space. Feel the weakening of the sub-personality as it comes into balance.

Allow the pink love energy of your Oversoul and God-Mind to fill any empty space that you may feel around you. This love will keep the other sub-personalities balanced as they adjust themselves to life without so much anger energy. Always give thanks for this process of inner balancing.

RELEASING GUILT: Using the above technique, allow the green healing energy of your Oversoul and God-Mind to fill any empty space that you may feel around you.

RELEASING FEAR: Using the above technique, allow the blue peaceful, calming energy of your Oversoul and God-Mind to fill any empty space that you may feel around you.

FORGIVENESS ON THE OVERSOUL LEVEL

I forgive myself for any harm that I have done to any person, animal, place, or thing, either intentionally or unintentionally, in this lifeline or in others. I ask them to forgive me via the involved Oversouls. I release any guilt that I consciously or unconsciously feel.

I forgive anyone who has harmed me, my friends and family, my animals, places, or things either intentionally or unintentionally, either in this lifeline or in others. I ask that I be released from any psychic cords that are no longer necessary; that these cords be dissipated on the inner levels.

I ask that any person needing help from these past actions, myself included, be sent the help each needs. I recognize that everyone was only playing a part in the grand play of life.

I give thanks for all experiences and the knowledge that they brought me. I return to you what came from you. I give thanks.

RELEASING EXCESS EGO

During your meditation, offer your ego up to your Oversoul. Give thanks for the lessons and the knowledge that it brought you. Explain that you do not know how much ego you still need, so you release it all. Ask that only what you need be returned to you.

Ask to be taught more about your ego, so that you understand its proper place in your life; so that you learn to use it without it using you. Ask that people and situations come into your life that validate your current level of development. Give thanks for the tools that strengthen your self-confidence, which in turn feed your self-esteem.

BALANCING THE POSITIVES

Breathe yourself into your center. Ask your Oversoul to show you the positive parts of Self that are too strong. Allow past experiences to come before your inner eye that are examples of what happens when positive parts are too strong. Identify the specific sub-personalities involved.

Ask your Oversoul to take the excess energy from these positive sub-personalities and return only what you need. Explain that you need inner balance; that you want compassion, understanding, kindness, etc., in your life, but they must be in balance to know what you and others need.

Recognize that too much of anything is damaging. Know that this proactive choice to consciously balance too strong positive sub-personalities protects you from inner pain at a later time. Finally, give thanks for the objectivity that balance brings. Release everything to your Oversoul.

GLOSSARY

AURA: Your personal energy field.

AFFIRMATION: A statement that defines a course of action, or a state of inner being; repeating words many times by thinking, speaking, or writing it to bring new avenues of action into your conscious mind.

CENTER: Your center is aligned along your spine, providing a safe space from which to work; you pull yourself into it by willing yourself into it.

COLLECTIVE CONSCIOUS MIND: The body of space that contains the accumu lated known knowledge of humankind.

COLLECTIVE UNCONSCIOUS: The body of space that contains the accumulated thoughts of humankind; these established thought patterns directly affect what you move through today.

CONSCIOUS MIND: Contains your present.

DIRECT AWARENESS: To know by experiencing the knowledge.

ENERGY: A physical substance consisting of shape, weight, consistency, and color.

GOD-MIND: Neutral energy; All That Is.

HABIT RESPONSE: An established pattern of behavior that allows you to react to any given situation without thinking, whether physical or mental, it can be positive, negative, or neutral.

HORIZONTAL EXPERIENCE: Pulls you out into similar growth.

ILLUSION: The way you perceive things to be.

KNOW BY KNOWING: To understand through direct awareness; to understand the feeling of an experience.

KNOWLEDGE: Information.

MACROCOSM: God-Mind; All That Is.

MEDITATION: A process that moves you beyond words and connects you with silence, the level of feeling.

MICROCOSM: You; a world in miniature.

NEGATIVE: Negative is not "bad," but merely a condition that exists; the opposite of positive, which explains another part of the same experience.

OBJECTIVE LISTENING: Listening and evaluating without judgment or criticism.

OBJECTIVE OBSERVING: Watching and evaluating without judgment or criticism.

OVERSOUL: Neutral energy that comes out of God-Mind; your Oversoul is to you what your Earth parents are to your body. Your Oversoul is your point of origin out of God-Mind.

POSITIVE: Positive is not better than negative, but is merely a condition that exists; the opposite of negative, which explains another part of the same experience.

PROACTIVE LEARNING: Active learning; gathering knowledge before an experience occurs.

PSYCHIC ENERGY: Your personal energy; it flows back and forth, and is horizontal.

REACTIVE LEARNING: Passive learning; gathering knowledge after an experience occurs.

REALITY: The way things really are; it may vary considerably from your perception of the way you think things are.

SILENCE: The deepest level of inner awareness; the level of feeling; you connect with your Oversoul and God-Mind within silence.

SPIRITUALITY: A state of inner being.

SUBCONSCIOUS MIND: Contains your memories, moment by moment, lifeline by lifeline.

SUB-PERSONALITY: A group of similar emotions that becomes strong enough to develop its own consciousness; a sub-personality is not you, but it is a part of you.

SUPERCONSCIOUS MIND: Provides the direct link to your Oversoul and God-Mind.

UNIVERSAL ENERGY: Energy that is available to everyone; using it allows you to keep your psychic energy; it flows up and down, and is vertical.

VERTICAL EXPERIENCE: Pulls you up into new growth.

VIBRATORY IMPRINT: Accumulated feelings of like experiences; they cause you to react to your experiences of today through your accumulated feelings of yesterday.

WISDOM: Knowledge applied.

YOU: Individualized neutral energy.

JOIN A LIFE SUPPORT GROUP™

LEARN TO EASILY FIND YOUR OWN ANSWERS!
Developed by Janet Swerdlow

EXPLORE: The most fascinating person you know: YOU!

UNDERSTAND: Mysticism, God-Mind, spirituality, positive/negative, universal/psychic energy, color/sound, Oversoul/soul communication, vertical/horizontal growth.

DEVELOP: Inner sight, intuition, Oversoul communication, discernment, leadership abilities—become a Life Support Group™
Leader in your area.

CHANGE: Self, relationships, career, finances, home.

INTERPRET: Your inner life to change the outer, your outer life to change the inner.

TOOLS: Group wisdom, toning, meditation, visualization, prayer, affirmations, stretching, mental exercises, Oversoul communication.

LIFE SUPPORT GROUP™ GOALS

To Clean Up The Past

To Be Able To Change

To Be Able to Move Forward

To Integrate Body, Mind, & Spirit

To Rely On Myself, Oversoul, & God-Mind

To Define Spirituality In A Way That Is Meaningful

To Accept Who I Am At This Moment In Time & Space

To Like Who I Am At This Moment In Time & Space

To Learn To Acquire Knowledge & The Wisdom To Use It Correctly

To Acknowledge & Assume Total Responsibility For Where I Am In My Life, Including Abundance, Relationships, Health, Environment, Finances, Career, & Personal Satisfaction

Life Support Group Testimonials

*"Working with **Decoding Your Life** is like remembering who and what you are after a long deep bout with amnesia."*
Maureen Martino, Life Support Group ™ Leader, New Jersey

"After my first encounter with Janet's writings I knew two things: her tools and incredible intuitive abilities/insights were catalysts for growth; and I wanted to be part of a Life Support Group ™ so I started one! Since then, using Janet's tools and insights, I have experienced great personal growth; and our still-young LSG™ provides the opportunity to share and grow with others, and to give and receive support at all levels. Janet has precious rare gifts that she shares abundantly. Love and thanks!" Patrica K., Life Support Group™ Leader, Idaho

*"**Decoding Your Life**" has provided me with the information that has helped me explore what my true potential really is."*
Susan Garguillo, Life Support Group™ Member

*"**Decoding Your Life** has been an eye-opening experience for me and enabled me to discover more about myself. This work inspiries me to become a more balanced human being."*
Bernadette Janovic, Life Support Group™ Member

*"Using my Oversoul has changed my life. I am working on changing my mind-patterns that I have learned and used since childhood. They were not working for me anymore. I found the answers through use of my Oversoul which is outlined in **Decoding Your Life** and our Life Support Group™ meetings."*
Bonnie Fogler, Life Support Group™ Member

*"I feel **Decoding Your Life** is very basic and user friendly, tying all of my metaphysical knowledge together in a very practical manner."*
Alana Wilson, Life Support Group™ Member

INDEX

www.janetswerdlow.com

Visit the *Expansions* website to read the
latest up-to-date information on:

Daily Practical Tips
Current Event & News Postings
Stewart's Column: *Stewart Says...*
Janet's Articles: *Belief Systems Shattered*
Janet's Column: *Dear Friends*
Dream Center
Life Support Group™ and Leader Contacts
Latest Books, Videos, & Products
Seminars, Lectures, & Events
Contributing Authors....and Much More!